I0141914

JUST
SOUTH
OF
FOREVER

JUST
SOUTH
OF
FOREVER

a collection of 23 inspirational
writings from the Gulf States
Christian Writers Association

❧

Compiled by
Mark Wyatt and Mary Ann Wyatt

WHP
Wyatt House Publishing
Mobile, Alabama
www.wyattpublishing.com

© Copyright 2013- Mark A. Wyatt/ GSCWA
All rights reserved. Permission is granted to copy or reprint portions
for any noncommercial use, except they may not be posted online
without permission.

Wyatt House books may be ordered through booksellers
or by contacting:

WYATT HOUSE PUBLISHING
399 Lakeview Dr. W.
Mobile, Alabama 36695
www.wyattpublishing.com
editor@wyattpublishing.com

*Because of the dynamic nature of the Internet, any web address or links
contained in this book may have changed since publication and may no
longer be valid. The views expressed in this book are solely those of the
author(s) and do not necessarily reflect those of the publisher, and the
publisher hereby disclaims any responsibility for them.*

Cover design by: Mark Wyatt

ISBN 13 TP: 978-0-9896119-0-9
Library of Congress Control Number: 2013911178

Printed in the United States of America

CONTENTS

Introduction

A Dad In Summer *by Mark Wyatt*   11

Not Enough Duct Tape *by Tamara Lee*   17

Love *by Lauren Paige Tate*   25

Bucket List *by Lauren Fenner*   31

The Gift of His Name *by Gabriel Walker*   35

Love's Revolution and other poems *by Kevin Cooley*   43

The Rental *by Mary Ann Wyatt*   49

A Storied Life *by Kenny Thacker*   61

A Picture *by Emily LaForce*   73

Life Lessons From the Road *by Jamie Harvill*   79

Revealing Responses *by Monica Warren*   85

A Dance With Eternal Impact *by Lonnie Honeycutt*   97

Arthur's Poem *submitted by David Brumbaugh*   107

Oldsmobile *by Gary Morris*   113

The Possum in the Road *by Stephen Simpson*   119

Sophia *by Candy Reid*   125

The Life of a Flower *by Jessica Laurie*   131

Weaving a Tapestry of Love *by Katie Stuckas*   137

Better Than Jesus *by Jennifer Lopes*   153

From Fear to Flight *by Pat Fenner*   163

Like Father, Like Son *by Mark Wyatt*   173

Psalms in Poetry *by Keith W. Currie*   185

Closing the Door *by Ramona Obrien*   197

"I miss your biscuits and your gravy
Fireflies dancing in the night
You have fed me, you have saved me,
Billy Graham and Martha White..."

Lyrics from "Southern Comfort Zone"
Brad Paisley/ Kelley Lovelace/ Chris DuBois

You Are Here...

Welcome to the first anthology from the Gulf States Christian Writers Association. We hope you find a breath of fresh air blowing in these pages. Some of the finest southern writing is right here, from new and talented authors who have something to say.

Some of the writings in this volume will be a warm summer breeze that will waft in from an unexpected window and will soothe away the tensions and pressures of your day. Some will be a gulp of fresh-squeezed lemonade made with pure cane sugar, that as soon as it goes down, it brings a grin to your face. And others will be a walk by a quiet stream, the oaky scent of old fallen leaves bringing fresh air into tired lungs.

The works you are about to read—these stories, these poems, these observations of the life that is grounded in a walk with God—are intended to whisper in your ear, to encourage you, to hold your hand for a few steps longer. You will see that some of these authors have been bursting with truth and good news and they can't wait for you to see what they have seen. Some of them will have a conversation with you over a piece of warm coffee cake as you listen to their stories. Still others, it will seem, are just thinking out loud with you in the room, relaxing in the quiet roar of a window unit air conditioner as the mysteries of eternity unfold before you.

I'm glad you're here. So, come on in and sink into the couch. You have arrived at one of the best places on earth. You are just south of forever.

Mark Wyatt
President, Wyatt House Publishing
and Gulf States Christian Writers Association
June 2013
Mobile, Alabama

A Dad In Summer

by Mark Wyatt

For at least that one week, we had him all to ourselves. Every Monday through Friday, Dad was designing bridges, buildings, and who knew what else for the Corps of Engineers all day long, but for one week and two whole weekends—one on either side of it— he was ours. As soon as school was out and summer was in, the family car was loaded and all seven of us would pile in for the four hour drive to Lake Martin. In the early years, it was the white station wagon with blue vinyl interior, but later it was the wide, yellow Ford LTD Galaxy 500 sedan. Except for that first summer when the LTD was brand new, and my mother backed into a fire hydrant in the Shopper's Fair parking lot after buying supplies for our vacation, which was to take place in our brand new car the next day. The car was creamed. Back to the white station wagon that year.

I liked traveling in both cars for different reasons. In the LTD, as the youngest and smallest of five children, I got to ride curled up in the back window. If I saw that today, I would call the police. In the station wagon it was cool to sit in the rear-facing jump seats and make faces at the people behind us. But when we took that car on vacation, the back was packed, so the only place I could stretch out was in the floorboard, among my siblings' dangling feet. That was okay, too, once you got used to the hump. And the places where the front seatbelts were fastened to the hump. Man, you had to watch out for those. I think I still have a tattoo branded on my hip in the shape of a 2-inch hexagon-headed bolt.

It was all worth it, though, because in four short hours, my father would manifest his one magic power. Somehow, he knew, every year, when we were exactly ten beats away from our destination. "10, 9, 8, 7..." and when he got to zero, we would turn off the main road and onto the long driveway to the cabin. We knew we had arrived, as we passed the little arrow-shaped sign that said "Whispering Pines," and heard the welcoming crunch of the large, smooth rocks that filled the two tire ruts, down a gentle hill, up another, curving to the right, turning left, to pull up at the door. After the unpacking and bladder relieving, our week on the water commenced.

Every year, I counted the number of boards on the pier, from the shore to the plywood deck at the end with the green canvas rope that served as some kind of rail, although I can't remember for the life of me what that number always was. What I do remember was how I stepped faster at the end because my feet were burning. We jumped a thousand times into the deep, green water from that pier each day, and floated inside enormous truck tire innertubes for hours on end, continually splashing cool water on the black rubber and trying not to get impaled by the three-inch long valve stem that always seemed to find its way around to your back.

But no matter how much fun the five of us kids were having, the excitement level went up when Mom and Dad came down to the pier. Mom would slather Coppertone over everyone again, but I think it was just fragranced hand lotion in a Coppertone bottle, because we all got sunburned just the same. Then Dad would dive in, and it seemed the most perfect dive ever performed. Granted it was only two feet from the edge of the pier into the water, but there was always so little splash that we figured that our father had a secret history of Olympic diving achievements that he just never told us about out of modesty.

During that week each summer, we would be awakened before dawn to motor away to the best fishing spots, and we would come back in a few hours to the smell of breakfast. After a few hours of swimming, we walked to Real Island Marina for Chocolate Snaps and Yoo-Hoos and Coke in glass bottles. When it rained, we laid on the bunk beds on the screened-in porch and watched it move across the lake like a curtain. On at least one afternoon, sometimes more, it was our job to assist with the homemade ice cream by one of us sitting on the freezer while Dad turned the crank, stopping periodically to smash up a frozen milk carton of ice with the side of a hammer. On other afternoons it was our grown up thrill to shoot his .22 pistol at cans on the hillside, or to unload a million BBs into ketchup bottles at the dump. At night, we fried the fish caught during the day, and caught lightning bugs in a jar as the starlit lake lapped against the shore. Then, back upstairs in the cabin, we played every kind of game imaginable—card games, board games, push-your-arms-into-the-doorframe-as-hard-as-you-can-for-thirty-seconds-and-watch-them-float-upward kind of games. My favorite of those was one night when I was about 6 years old. I was blindfolded and told that I was going to take a magic carpet ride. My siblings sat me on a wide, sturdy board and flew me around the room, until I bumped my head on the ceiling, which was actually just a dictionary that one of them held just above my head. For years I was convinced I had flown.

It has only recently occurred to me that those times at Lake Martin were only seven or eight days long, but when I talk about it, I find myself telling people that I "spent my boyhood summers" on the Lake. Today, my most powerful memories of summer swirl around that time and place; the fragrant pines, the fresh, clean smell of the lake, the distant thrum of boats, the small splash of a perfect dive, the night songs of a hundred frogs, the Carpenters, Bread, and Seals and Crofts rising from the tinny speakers of a Panasonic portable tape recorder on a gloriously hot afternoon on the pier. And I know the reason why my memories stay tethered there. Because that was where we were all together. My mother has since passed away, we all now have families of our own, and the cabin was sold years ago.

And now I am a Dad in Summer. A few days ago, I taught my daughter how to ride a bike in a local park. A few weeks ago, we had homemade ice cream at my brother's house, and nobody had to sit on the freezer. My wife and children and I spent a week in a house at Gulf Shores, where there is a store that smells just like Real Island Marina and sells Yoo-Hoos and Coke in glass bottles. During the day, we swim together, and at night we watch the sunset, cook fish, and play all kinds of games. And we are all together.

The last time I was near the Lake, I took my family to see where my summers had been made. I counted down from ten and turned off the main road, and heard the crunch of rocks under the tires. The "Whispering Pines" sign is long gone, but I followed the drive down the hill, up another, right, then left. I could hardly see the house behind the overgrowth. It sat, solitary and neglected and I noticed that part of the roof had caved in. It was the same roof, I remember, that I bumped my head on one night when I took a magic carpet ride. And somewhere, on a warm summer evening, that house is still there, with the lingering smell of supper, laughter ringing against the walls, and the easy comfort of nowhere else to be. It is there, in my childhood, where we are all still together.

CR

Dr. Mark Wyatt is a native of Mobile, Alabama, and he and his wife, Mary Ann, have four children: Samuel, Sarah, Nathaniel, and Autumn. Mark is the founding and senior pastor of Deeper Life Fellowship in Mobile. He holds a Bachelor's degree from Auburn University, a Master's degree from Southwestern Baptist Theological Seminary, and a Ph.D. in Biblical Studies from Atlantic Coast Theological Seminary. He is the author of *The New Normal: Experiencing the Unstoppable Move of God* (Destiny Image, Shippensburg, PA, 2011); *Hog Washed: a small fable about a big change* (Wyatt House Publishing, Mobile, AL, 2012); and "Honey, I'm Home!: a one-act play" (Contemporary Drama Service, Colorado Springs, CO, 2013). Dr. Wyatt also serves as the founder and president of the Gulf States Christian Writers Association (www.gulfstatescwa.org). You can follow his blog at www.drmarkwyatt.com, and he invites you to friend him on facebook.

NOT ENOUGH DUCT TAPE

by Tamara Lee

There will be days when I'm feeling particularly deep and spiritual and will want to share it. This will not be one of them.

I bought the duct tape for a secret project I was going to tackle while my husband was out of town last week, but I never got around to it. This is actually a very good thing.

First, a little background. I have a one track mind. By this I mean that when I get an idea, I can't think about anything else. The idea is the fox and I'm the bloodhound. That's background fact #1. Background fact #2 is that lately, and by lately I mean starting in 1996, I've become obsessed with my weight. I lost almost 30 lbs last summer. During Christmas, I gained 10 of them back.

By March I'd lost them again. Now here we are in June and those pesky 10 have picked up 2 more. I have never gotten the hang of eating properly. I like to say that it's because until age 26, I didn't have to. I don't think God plays fair. He lets you eat fast food for the first half of your life without consequence, and then suddenly you land a man and that cute little size 4 red plaid dress you were wearing the first time your husband noticed you won't go past your hips. What's that about? And don't get me started on gravity. But I digress. That's another day.

Another background fact is that I'm an instant gratification kinda gal. I started cutting my own hair years ago when I couldn't get in to see my fabulous Las Colinas stylist on the same day my bangs went rogue. I have no patience.

Which brings us to last week. I'd stood in front of the mirror a thousand times too many and imagined what it would look like if I could take a knife and whack off the parts I didn't like. Enough was enough. If liposuction isn't in my future, then there has to be a Plan B. And it has to happen now. So off to the hardware store I went.

I heard the rattle of the bag from the other room. "Mom, what are you gonna do with this?" I couldn't tell them the truth, so it was time to make that decision. You know the one: do I lie to my children or tell them the truth and reveal that their mother is a crazy bloodhound? I went for the former. Mother of the Year would have to wait.

By the time I had gotten around to putting my plan into action, it was Sunday morning and my husband was home. But he was still asleep, so I thought I was good. I'm always the first one up on Sundays. I got my stool and put it in front of the bathroom mirror, got my scissors and my new shiny roll of duct tape, and off I went. I started at the afore-mentioned hip area. Three times around should do it. I started to put on my skirt when I heard him. You see, I hadn't realized how much noise I was making. Not only is duct tape loud, but it makes an unmistakable sound. Especially to the ears of a handy man like mine. "What are you doing?" I ignored it. I was finished anyway. He'll go back to sleep. I got my skirt on. From the front, perfection. I had done it. I had lobbed off my upper thighs without a knife. I stepped off the stool and got my shoes. I went out into the bedroom and he looked up.

"What are you doing?"

"Nothing. I'm leaving. See you soon," I whispered.

At this point, for reasons unknown except that God actually does love me, I casually ran my hands across the back of my skirt. I can't really describe what I felt except to say it was some sort of new development. Like a growth. A big roll where there had never, ever been one before. I went back into the bathroom and got back on the stool. I turned to check the rear view when I saw it. There was this....shelf. I hadn't realized it, but all that stuff I was binding had to go somewhere, and it went up, in a terribly unattractive place. My rear. Not a problem. I dropped my skirt (which fell off effortlessly, what with me having just lost 3 inches and all) and grabbed the tape again. I started at the problem area and went around a few times when I heard it again. "What are you doing?" I checked the clock and kept going. Sound check was fast approaching and I did not have time to answer these ridiculous questions at 7:40 in the morning. Can't a woman get ready for church without interruptions? I put my skirt back on. This time I didn't have to turn around. The shelf had moved to my waist. And only on one side. I looked like a hunchback who couldn't even get that right. I inched my way around on the stool to check the back to see what was going on. This was not good. While the mid-rear shelf was gone, other things had gone south. I grabbed the tape and started again. This was getting complicated. The lower I had to go, the harder it was going to be to walk. I don't have time for this! Glancing at the clock again I was in full panic mode. I was wrapping faster than an elf on Christmas Eve, tossing the tape from one hand to the other. I'd developed quite a rhythm. After more than a few times around at this super pace, I had the lower problem solved. Awesome. I'll have to take really small steps but I can do this. I'll just make sure no one's behind me when we're walking up the steps to get on stage. No big deal. I continued upward to address the issue on the side. 'I wonder if it will hurt to take this off? Not now, Tamara. Beauty is pain. And at least you're not working up a sweat putting on your Spanx.' This was a wonderful thought. I wasn't going to need another shower after putting on an undergarment. Fueled by this enthusiasm I went faster. His voice was getting louder now but I couldn't be bothered with explanations. I kept going. And going. My entire mid and lower sections were bound. Good thing my shirt was black. But what was up with my knees? All that stuff had been smushed down to my legs! But my skirt was long enough. I just won't be able to cross my legs. I can still make this work. OK time to assess. Let's see what we've got. I tossed the roll on the counter and went for the skirt. That's when I realized the flaw in my plan. I had managed to bind all my unwanted parts quite successfully, but I hadn't factored in actually being able to get down from the stool. Or breathing. I couldn't do either. Dang it, if I could just get the skirt on - it will hang so cute, I just know it! (Remember the one track mind thing?) But there was no way. I was literally stuck, 12 inches off the ground, in front of my mirror, looking at this ridiculous image of myself covered in grey. And then it happened. "TAMARA! What are you DOING?!" He wasn't going to be ignored anymore. And the terrible cursed fact was, I needed him.

As I was calling for him I started to try to get it off. This is when I discovered that duct tape is not only loud, but terribly sticky. In fact, terribly doesn't cut it. And neither do scissors when it's attached to your underwear.

"HELP!" I yelled. "I can't get out!" He came through the

bathroom door. He didn't stop to ask. He didn't even look surprised. Because he wasn't. He had known all along what I was doing. The man lived with me. It didn't take a genius.

He sat down on the edge of the bathtub and started to cut me out of my duct tape tomb. I was clawing at the front. "Strings??!! It's -- there's all these -- it turns into strings?? I can't -- it didn't work!!" He was just nodding and smiling. "I know babe. I know."

Miraculously and sweetly, he freed me. He even spared the Victoria's Secret underwear from a single clip. And me & my hips made it to sound check on time.

I noticed a little piece of tape on the stage that morning and had to chuckle. OK, I didn't chuckle. I threw up in my mouth a little, and then I tried not to cry.

But today, with about 96 hours between me and my statue, I think I've actually learned something. I know it won't work. I no longer have to be obsessed and preoccupied. There is no instant gratification when it comes to hippage. Starving myself last summer did absolutely no good because I couldn't keep it up. Having 28 less pounds of me was wonderful while it lasted, but the obsessive way I got there was not maintainable. And when I was finished, there was still a McDonald's on every corner and a Snickers at every Target checkout. I still say God doesn't play fair, but that belief hasn't gotten me very far in this particular area. So now I can move on to reasonable things like eating salad for dinner and spending more quality time with Eva The Elliptical and Tony the P90X man. Go figure.

❧

Tamara Lee currently resides in Arlington, Texas. She is a stay-home mom of two daughters, a grown son, one husband and 3 dogs. She is actively involved in the student ministry of her church where she and her husband teach together, and she home schools her 12 and 14 year old girls. If you'd like to read more of her blog, you can do so at www.expressivelee. blogspot.com.

LOVE

by Lauren Paige Tate

As a thought on your mother's heart, you experience love for the first time. As a child in your mother's womb, you experience love for the first time. As a baby born in the hospital room, laid on your mother's chest, you experience love for the first time. As a young child begging for that new doll in the store, whom you promise to love and adore, you experience love for the first time. You play and idolize your new piece of gold with all of your heart. Only to forget just a few months later the love you once had for the raggedy doll left on the floor. A new item has caught your eye and your love has run out for an older obsession.

As a preteen, your experience your first crush. Your first puppy love. He is dreamy and picks the fire out of you. You love being around him, you love writing to him as you pass notes through class. Soon, he becomes your boyfriend and you feel wanted, loved, pretty, and smart. You experience love for the first time. Soon enough though, you already know the story. He becomes old and not so flashy and exciting. A new boy has caught your eye. Or maybe you have been rejected. You both move on and grow up. You move on to high school, surrounded by parties and fun. You meet him. You just know that he is the one. He is what all the songs you have been hearing are singing about. He is all that you have ever dreamed about since childhood. He overpowers you, and sends a shock through your veins. You experience it. You experience him. You experience the dates, dances, proms, movies, fights, hurt, pain, jealousy, the brokenness. You experience him, this human who fails you daily. You put him on a pedestal. He rules your life, your emotions. He rules your day. And then it is over. It is over in an instant. All of the emotions, love, happiness, obsessions, and sadness that you have put into this relationship, is over. Over in an instant. And just like that, love has failed you. This first love experience has failed you. You turn to parties, you turn to highs. You turn to friends. You turn to beauty, you try and try to be someone that you physically and mentally cannot possibly be. It is impossible. You stress over who you are NOT and begin to lose your sense of who you ARE! You are loved. You turn to alcohol. You constantly look for new experiences. New love. Something new to capture your eye, your mind and soul. Something to make you feel whole. You are empty. Pretty soon, all of the bands, shows, friends, boys, clothes, money, drinks, and parties, overpower the noticeable need for attention in your life. The love you need, you cannot find. You, in moments, find yourself fulfilled . This feels good, only in that moment. I feel good. I feel love. It may not be the love that I thought I was looking for but I have found things that make me feel good and fulfilled for a moment. And that moment in itself is enough. You ravish in these moments of lust, whether it be physical or emotional. Whether it be bright and beautiful, whether it be dark and cold. You seek to find love, real love, no matter the cost.

This was me and this is where I had it all wrong. Real, true love was right in front of my face. My whole life I was searching for love. Trying to find it in all the wrong places. Filling my time up with useless, material things. I gave my life to Jesus as a young child, not truly understanding the meaning of the cross. I was not fully aware of the love that was available for me. A love that whether I accepted it or not and captured the full potential of this love, He loved me. He loves me.

I eventually had gotten to an all time low in my life. I was at a fork in the road. Do I go left or right? To the left of me stood a life of outward happiness and inward sadness. A life of physical highs and emotional lows. A life of the "day after depressions and daily obsessions." And to the right of me stood a life that was never promised to be easy, but a life of love. A life of forgiveness. A life of fulfillment and promise. Hope and understanding. He saw every mistake I had ever made and he loves me. I can be washed clean and made anew. I choose to turn right at the fork in the road. I choose to accept this love. I chose for this first time love experience to be never ending, continuously growing.

I couldn't find it in a human. I couldn't find this love in worldly possessions. People and worldly possessions will fail me every single day. My relationships, my parents, my children, my job, my social life. It will fail me. It did fail me. Yet, God tells us that no matter how far we run or how deep we go, His love is never ending. His love is an ocean that is overflowing. His love never fails . As I was a child in my mother's womb, I was His love. His pride and joy. He never is sick of me and tosses me to the side for something new. He loves me today more than he loved me yesterday. And tomorrow he will love me more than today. He makes all things new. He does not keep records of wrongs. He knew when he created me that I would be a sticky, stubborn, sinful mess. That was and is the point and the heart of his love for me.

With this newfound understanding of love, I want to share this love. The Father's love. I want as many people as I can reach to know the love that is available to them. No matter how far they are or have been, they need to know that like a lost sheep, one out of 100 in his flock. He will leave the 99 just to pursue and rescue you. He never gives up, his love never runs out for you. You are that important to him. You are his love.

"This is real love--not that we loved God, but that he loved us and sent his Son as sacrifice to take away our sins."

1 John 4:10

CR

Lauren Paige Tate lives in New Albany, Mississippi with her husband Zach and their two children Grayson who is 5 and Mary Ellen "Ellie" who is 9 months old. Lauren Paige worked, until recently, for Etta B Pottery as a potter and painter, when she and Zach decided it was more important for her to be home. She enjoys raising laying hens, gardening and selling homemade treats from both endeavors every weekend at the local farmers market. She also recently received a grant from the State of Mississippi to grow a community garden with children from the local Boy's and Girl's Club. She is a city girl raised in Mobile, Alabama who at 23 years old has found great joy in living a slower, small town life. In addition to raising children and chickens she is currently writing a blog for speakgreenmississippi.com.

BUCKET LIST

by Lauren Fenner

Do you ever think about the term "bucket list"? I often do. I like to think that everyone has a bucket list - things that they want to do before they die - even if they don't admit it or have it specifically written down.

And if you had asked me a couple of months ago what my bucket list was, I would have said the expected adventurous, out-of-the-box things that you would look for on a bucket list - live and travel throughout Europe, backpack South America, write a book, dance competitively. But recently, I had an experience that really opened my eyes and gave me a very different perspective.

Through an unexpected series of events, a few months ago I found myself sitting behind bars in the city jail. Although I had done nothing wrong, I ended up spending the night there, and dealing with months of legal proceedings after the fact. Although the Lord eventually sorted out my issues, I can't help thinking about the other people that I met and left behind in that jail, the people who have so much more pain and heartache in their lives than I've ever had in mine.

And that brings me back to my thoughts on bucket lists. My time in jail made me realize how shallow my goals are. I mean sure, it'd be cool if I got to do all of those things - they're activities that I love to do, and that I want to experience as much of as I can. But after I die, will it matter?

After I die, who will really care if I've backpacked throughout South America? Perhaps my friends who survive me, maybe my children, will talk about it as a way of sort of living vicariously through me, or to keep my memory alive. But after they are gone? Who will remember what I've done? Not meaning to sound morbid, but the truth is that no one will. No one will remember. No one will care.

Oxford dictionary defines a bucket list as "a number of experiences or achievements that a person hopes to have or accomplish during their lifetime". But why does it have to end there? Why do we only aspire for things that will affect the goings-on of our own lives, perhaps the lives of our children, and then end? We were created to make an everlasting impact, to have an effect on eternity. So why do we regulate ourselves to the tiny window of 70-80 years on this earth that we have been given to effect change??

A bucket list is, essentially, an investment in one's own life. It's a list of things that you want to do so that your life is enriching and fulfilling and so that you are happier and more successful. But life is meant to be so much more than about just ourselves!! As a teacher, I am learning anew every day the sublime joy, the supreme happiness that results from serving others. From living not only for yourself, but rather from making other people your first priority. There are so many hurting souls all around us – the homeless, the ill, the incarcerated. And yet, so often, we ignore their hurt and submerse ourselves into our own selfish lives. But God has called us to a higher purpose; a more noble bucket list, if you will.

And here's the best part. Investing in others is not only personally rewarding, but eternally rewarding. It's the only way, really, to make a difference that will outlive your lifetime, and the lifetime of your descendants...even the lifetime of the very world. So what kind of bucket list will you have? Will you have one that gratifies yourself and yourself only, and will die with you? Or will you have one that serves others, and will be remembered for all of eternity? I don't know about you, but after my night in jail, that's not a very difficult choice to make. I pray that most people don't need to spend an evening behind bars to learn where their priorities should lie.

☙

Lauren Fenner is a writer, traveler, dancer, and life enthusiast. Her writings have been published on travel websites such as bravoyourcity.com, as well as print publications such as *Erato*, the arts and literature magazine of Georgia Institute of Technology. After graduating with a dual Bachelor's degree in Spanish and Economics, she spent a year in South Korea on a Fulbright scholarship. She is currently studying for her Master's degree in International Affairs at Georgia Tech, while also working as a teaching assistant and writer for the school website. Having been to over a dozen countries – and lived in 3 of them – in less than 5 years, Lauren is passionate about seeing new places, experiencing new things, and expanding her world. In her mind, there is no such thing as a boring life – you just have to have the creativity to find the beauty in the mundane!

THE GIFT OF HIS NAME

by Gabriel Walker

Apparently, my Heart has adopted a theme as of late, not entirely with my permission. My musings and ponderings have been consumed with the "ties that bind." I am referring to Undying Love and Unbridled Devotion—the pieces of ethereal thread that God uses to sew hearts and lives together. Stated simply, my mind has been occupied with the idea of Marriage. It's a little unnerving to be honest. I mean, these are pretty heavy thoughts for a man in my social position (employed, no kids, single and not courting anyone's daughter). I'm not sure how I stumbled into this realm of thought, but it seems as if I might be here for awhile. That being said I ask your indulgence.

Gift giving is a practice that is held in high esteem amongst lovers (I do not mean the base interpretation of the word but the definition pertaining to sentiment). Tokens of appreciative affection are often used to gauge the progress and subsequent success of a romantic relationship. One such (notable) gift is the engagement ring. And there is an unhealthy myth affixed to the engagement ring--that price paid is directly proportional to the level of devotion of the giver. Please, do not misunderstand me. Engagement rings are exciting and I would not tarnish the ideals associated with their purchase and presentation. I look forward to presenting an engagement ring to some lucky woman one day, God willing. However, I believe that there is something far more valuable than a trinket of gold, silver, and jewels. What could possibly carry more weight than a dazzling multi-carat diamond ring? One's Name. Am I insane? Perhaps, I am. But I am going to reference my relationship with Jesus Christ in an attempt to prove my sanity. Yes, I said Jesus Christ. The Son of God, the Savior of the World, the Prince of Peace, you know the One. Again, I ask your indulgence.

I will begin the argument for my sanity with the following: Jesus pledged Himself to me when He died on the Cross. His death upon the cross was suffered as an act of His love and devotion for me and for you. His selfless sacrifice served as a token of His love. As a kiss is oft given as a token of affection so Jesus' death was given as a token of His love for us. In His death we were offered a token, a gift, a pledge. Jesus' death was truly a romantic gesture, in my eyes. The romantic practice of giving a pledge token to one's beloved has faded into obscurity. In common

Gabriel Walker

practice a pledge token was usually an article of cloth or a favored personal affect. I mention this to make an observation: in this exchange it was often understood that the more personal the article, the more sincere the promise. Nothing is more personal than blood. Jesus shed His blood for me and for you thus showing the gravity of His Promise to us. Jesus Loved us so much that He died for us, literally (this is not said in jest but in truth).

A pledge token was a gift of promised Intent—the intent to pursue one's beloved emotionally with the goal of marriage in mind. Bear in mind that proffer of a gift does not guarantee acceptance. That is to say that love, no matter how earnest and pure, may go unrequited. Remember that (all) relationships require an agreement to walk together and in the same direction (see Amos 3:3). A pledge token merely lent physical form and/or expression to an offer of emotional commitment. Recall that I regard Jesus' death as a pledge token, an act of selfless love and devotion to the end of expressing both His emotional commitment and His devotion to me and to you.

Romantic emotional commitment is often developed over a period time. By modern convention this is established by dating. By dating I mean the quest for compatibility in the form of a series of scheduled meetings between you and an interesting party of the opposite sex usually involving food and/or entertainment of some sort. While most people of my generation submit to this practice I admire the more noble-in my opinion- pursuit of Courtship.

Dating has become a means to escape the social stigma of being single. By contrast, I find the purpose of courtship as such: to show and share the benefits of a life-long relationship with your beloved. And true courtship is a life-long process. It begins well before the giving of the pledge token and continues (God willing) for the duration of the marriage. That being said, I submit that Jesus' life and ministry served as His courtship of my soul. Every sermon, miracle, and wonder performed by Jesus on earth served as a glimpse of how a lifetime with Him would be. Through the gospels we are treated to numerous accounts of Jesus as a Healer and Teacher and Provider. We are also given, through the gospels, a glimpse of the kind of man Jesus is. The time that Jesus spent with the disciples was not an escape from the monotony of the day, rather it was an engaging experience that served to prepare them (and also us) for a lifelong relationship with Him. Jesus' ministry on Earth was a measured and intentional courtship.

The purpose of courtship is to show and share the benefits of a lifelong relationship. Courtship also serves as a preparatory stage for Marriage. By common convention –in most western countries- a marriage ceremony is preceded by a marriage proposal. Speaking as a single male, the marriage proposal is a huge deal. I'm not talking about the timing and place of actually "popping the question." No, I am talking about the gravity of the proposal, the meaning of it. The traditional question "Will you marry me?" is the most revealing question that a man can ask a woman. In asking this a man is truly asking numerous questions in one. "Am I enough for you? Do you Trust me? May I Love you with all that I am? Do you want a Life with me, regardless of circumstance?" These four are only a sampling of the myriad questions contained within "Will you marry me?"

When a marriage proposal is accepted, several wonderful and exciting things happen. Plans are made. Friends are gathered together. Families are merged and lives are blended together for the Glory of God. Something else, of great import, happens as well. The potential for change is formed. When two lives are blended together through holy matrimony, addresses may change, possessions may be trimmed, and names may change. The potential change of greatest impact, in my opinion, is the potential name change. Your name is, in a sense, what you're worth. Think about it. Our educational, judicial, and financial records are all filed using names. We use numbers to help us out, but the core of a person's identity is their name. A good name is a valuable thing! (See Proverbs 22:1.) If a woman marries a man with a bad (ill-reputed) name, she could gain his bad name. And, if a woman marries a man with a good (well-regarded) name, she may gain it as well.

I've mentioned Jesus' courtship of my soul and His pledge to you and to me by His blood. Did Jesus propose marriage to me as well? Yes. Yes, He did. And He proposed to you, too. When Jesus ascended into Heaven He wasn't just going Home. He was making a proposal, a proposal of Eternity. During His life, Jesus demonstrated the benefits and the Power of His name. Upon His Ascension, Jesus demonstrated the Glory and Majesty of His name. Jesus told the twelve disciples that He was going away to prepare a place for them, and, consequently, for us as well. (See John 14:1-4) In times past, when a man was really serious about getting married, he prepared a house for his betrothed. He began courtship of his lady fair, confessed his love for her, presented her with a pledge token which communicated his commitment and intentions, and then he made preparations to provide for his beloved. Sometimes the bridegroom had to depart to another town or country to secure a place for himself and his bride to be. And when all was in readiness, the groom came to claim his betrothed, his beloved bride and take her unto himself. Does that sound like anyone we know? Yes. Yes, it does. It sounds a lot like Jesus to me.

When I accepted Jesus as my Lord and Savior I said, "Yes," to His proposal of Eternity. I accepted Him for who He is. I gave Him my Trust. I wanted to live a Life with Him regardless of circumstance. I saw Love and delighted in Him! I discarded my name for His. I became His and He became mine. (See Song of Solomon 6:3a.) By giving me His name, Jesus placed upon me worth that only He could bring. His Name is my most precious possession. His Name is the gift I could never repay, the gift that I will always treasure. What does this have to do with one's name being worth more than an engagement ring? In answer I turn to a cultural reference made in Song of Solomon 1:2-3:

> *2 Let him kiss me with the kisses of his mouth! For your love is better than wine; 3 your anointing oils are fragrant; your name is oil poured out; therefore virgins love you."* (ESV)

These verses are "spoken" by the bride portrayed. This woman is saying that her husband is such a blessing to her, that he has become her most valued asset. His very presence is a pleasure to her. When she says, "your name is oil poured out...," she is giving him the highest compliment that a married woman could give her husband. A paraphrase: "The man that you are is so Amazing to me! I am glad to share your name! You bring worth to me. I am the envy of unmarried women because of you, because I have your name."

Notice the bride doesn't boast about the groom's wealth or gifts. She boasts about his name. She praises him for sharing his name with her. The sentiment that is expressed by the portrayed bride for her husband is the same feeling that my Heart has towards Jesus Christ. As believers in Christ, we often speak of Praising His Holy Name and of thanking Him for what He has done for us. This passage also evokes a goal within me: to foster this same feeling in the woman I will marry. I want her to feel this way about me. I want to be a man of God that exemplifies the Worth that I have received from the Name of Christ Jesus in every aspect of my life, especially in my marriage. I want my life, every day that remains, to be a token of appreciation. I could never repay what was Given to me, nor would I attempt to. I simply want to live a life of Thanksgiving.

He is High and Lifted up; Forever shall He Reign

His is my Portion and I am His Claim

Let us Praise The Lord Our God

For the Gift of His Name

ᔆ

Gabriel Walker lives and works in Mobile, Alabama. He enjoys reading the Bible and writing poems. Gabriel hopes to one day become an established Christian author with works in poetry and fiction. Currently, Gabriel works as a registered respiratory therapist in the neonatal intensive care unit at the University of South Alabama.

LOVE'S REVOLUTION
AND OTHER POEMS

by Kevin W. Cooley

Sometimes my spirit groans
When I'm alone
    And I let it
compassion flows
But I don't know
    I confess it
Just come & show
And I will go
    I am someone's deliverance!
It is my call
Don't let me fall
    Because of my own ignorance.
Am I Justice?
  Do I love it?
    Can I be it?

Just South of Forever

I may die
But by persistence
        I will try to see it!

Teach my hands to make war!
     Help my eyes see the door
Break down this Resistance!

Deep in my heart I know...
        It breaks; it flows
               for this existence:
Something more... beyond me
    That only Love can see
        Courage is the needed skill.
On distant shore... tears respond to me.
Longings to be free
        Faith still moves hills
So let it begin
    Let it be done
Each day before setting sun
Let my life count -
       Here's my contribution:
LOVE'S REVOLUTION!
Let it build
    Let it swell
Let us give
    And bankrupt hell!
No more taking; only Passion's aching

with open hands to all God's lands
and with open souls let us tell
                              What must be told
So if one day we are old
                         the world will know
we were here. We made a difference...
We were someone's deliverance!
Consumed in the flame; our ashes spread upon it's tide
History forgetting our name
                         but even though dead
                                        still speaking
far and wide
The groaning of the Spirit
                         and our children's children will
whisper, "I can still hear it!"
And when Tyranny comes
                         again to strike
the Seed that still glows will ignite
                              Freedom's Song
and all who long
            for good
                    will hear it
And like the Phoenix from the ashes
                              Love will rise
and Justice crashes
                  upon a generation
all creation will bow
                  and sing praise & veneration
for all who tried...

some lived, some died...
to give us these days again the world knows
Love is still alive!
Love's rEVOLution

LIFE'S A ROAD

Memories and destinies
That's what life is made of
Situations and inspirations
Send you searching for love

Strangers become the friends
Of lost and lonely wanderers
Broken boys become the sons
Of lost and wandering fathers

Life's a road, lighted by the stars.
See the rose, humbled by her scars.
Feel the wind, blowing through my hair
There's a friend that's Who's always been there

Visions of hope and dreams of fire
treasure somewhere out there
But really what we are searching for
Is a moment to share

Kevin W. Cooley

And in the moment passion can't pay
The jailer's cruel ransom
Then our eyes begin to see
What is truly handsome

How can we drink Life's water
Until we know life's like a Father
How can we love someone else
Until we learn to love ourselves

Life's a Road
Lighted by the stars
See the Rose
Humbled by her scars
Feel the Wind
Blowing through your hair
There's a Friend
Who will always be there

Wounded Eagle

It's difficult for me to explain
Though thought be my paint
Though words be my brush

The ideas somehow slip away
And I find myself surrounded

Just South of Forever

By the angry hush
But I do yearn to tell you
The things I fear I never can
The refrain my soul can barely sing

So again I'll gently hold you
With the strength you showed me
marveling at the wonder of this broken thing

Each day you amaze me
More than the one before
How you soar... on that broken wing

You took love's coin and chances bought
Though always thankful I'll wonder why
Like an angel you picked me up and taught
A wounded eagle how to fly

☙

Pastor Kevin Cooley has served in full-time ministry for over 20 years, graduated from mutliple Bible colleges, has traveled to more than 17 different nations to preach the Gospel, been involved in both children's and youth ministry, and is happily married to his wife Adrienne. Together, Kevin and Adrienne lead Harvest Church in Mobile, Alabama. They have two boys and enjoy jogging, reading, playing music, and meeting new people.

THE RENTAL

by Mary Ann Wyatt

From the thud against the wall, the pan must have been cast iron—not some lower class clangy metal like aluminum. I imagined it held some traditional southern after-church Sunday dinner food like fried chicken or pork chops. A loud, shrill, steady but somehow unintelligible screaming accompanied the thud. The crescendo was what I surmised were some kind of Chinette plates—as they didn't make a tell-tale shattering noise-- being hurled right behind the fried meat. A young girl crying left no doubt that there was a black storm cloud over the little brown house. I sat wordlessly on my banana seat bicycle rocking it slightly—forward, back, forward back-- in my driveway—wondering if I should go tell my mother. In the end, I decided that even in my ten year old mind, this was one of those low, ugly parts of human nature that was best experienced from a little distance—almost in a detached sort of way—like one would observe animals in a zoo or the results of some scientific experiment. Speaking the words out loud to my mother about what I was hearing would somehow bring those people and those actions into my world and I wanted them kept safely in theirs. Even if it was only the 15 feet or so that separated our carports and kitchen windows.

Over the many years we lived next door to what I would later in life call "The Rental," I got to observe a lot of the circus of human nature. Its beautiful, colorful parade followed by the three ring extravaganza. It was sometimes exciting, sometimes dull--and once in a while, in all the frenzy, the clowns turned just a little bit creepy. All was seen from that ever-so-slight distance—the width of two carports and a small strip of grass—so that their color and occasional creepiness didn't bleed onto my little family in our own little brown house. In a way, it was like moving somewhere different every year--different faces, different atmosphere, different neighborhood children-- while still keeping all the stability of my own school and my best friend 5 houses down and my own sky blue bedroom with the checked ruffled curtains and parquet wooden floor. I suppose it was the best of both worlds for a little girl who was stuck in one place but loved to watch and analyze people.

The meat-throwing woman was named Amanda. She was petite with short blond hair and even before the frying pan incident, demonstrated an insincere and somewhat unstable personality. Her husband was the opposite in appearance and demeanor. Kevin was tall, dark-haired, affable and seemed as safe as a teddy bear. My parents said many times he had left a "good-paying job at the post office" to become a preacher. Yes, they lived in The Rental because they had sold their house somewhere up north and he had come down to Mobile to get a degree in theology at the Baptist college. They had two young daughters, the oldest of which was tall dark-haired, sincere and affable like her father. The younger was small, blond, manipulative and a cry-baby. I knew as I sat on my bicycle that Sunday afternoon that Kevin was the recipient of the high pitched screaming and durable plastic plates. The younger girl was the one hysterically crying, and I pictured the older one sitting bewildered and silent at the kitchen table. I realized over the year or two they lived next door that this was probably not a one-time event and I thought, even at ten, that Kevin was going to have to spend a lifetime cleaning up after her. Whatever being a Baptist preacher's wife looked like, she was not cut out for it.

Before my parents ever met and married, my mother bought the house in which we lived as a single working woman. This was not a common occurrence in 1962. Back then, the neighborhood was a brand new development of small working-class ranch-style homes not too far from the interstate. The original owners of The Rental next door were a young couple with a baby. When the husband finished law school, they moved on to bigger and better things. I was never sure whether they kept ownership of the house or sold it to someone else. I did know the owners never came around themselves. Just that steady stream of renters.

The first family that I remember living in The Rental moved in several years before the Baptist preacher trainee and his nervous wife. This was back when I was too young to go very far from my mother's eyes at our kitchen window and I rode a little red tricycle around my carport instead of my banana-seat bicycle. I remember the dad in that family most of all. He was large and boisterous and had longer hair than I had ever seen on a man. The only memory I have of his wife was that she was as the adults said, "heavy-set." They had a lot of children of different ages. It seemed like about ten but in reality was probably 4 or 5. For a few months in the summer of 1969, however, the number of children in that little 800 square foot house did number a dozen. Long-Haired Dad worked up the road at the Lion gas station. I was never sure why it was called that because it was, in fact, a Gulf station. One day, a large family of what others in the neighborhood called gypsies apparently coasted into the Lion station on fumes with about 6 small starving children. Long-Haired Dad apparently had a big heart as well so he brought them down into the neighborhood to The Rental to feed them some sandwiches for lunch. Supper came around and they stayed for that. Then he couldn't just send them all back on the road with no place to sleep so they stayed the night. And the next day and the next week and the next month.

I was fascinated by all those dark-haired children. There were so many and all of them skinny with worn clothes and dirty fingernails. I know now I had never seen poverty like that before and probably seldom since. We, and the others on our little street, were in no way rich but I always had plenty of food and a pretty little twin bed all to myself and a pretty mom who kept me meticulously clean like it or not. I remember one hot afternoon, one of the little girls—probably my age or younger—cut her dirty little foot in the yard and was screaming and screaming. From the safety of my carport, I could see all the adults gathered around her while they held her foot in the kitchen sink and tried to pull out a shard of glass that was embedded in her heel. After her wailing finally subsided, I heard one curse and say they would never have believed that so large a piece of glass could have gone so deep in such a small foot. I remember never being so glad—for many reasons—I was not that little gypsy girl. The father of the gypsy children was apparently some kind of artist and Long-Haired Dad fed and housed Artist-Dad's children for a month in exchange for an enormous hand-painted yellow lion with brown mane and "Lion Gas Station" in bright red letters that he painted on its plate glass window. It regally watched over the entrance to our little neighborhood for many years afterward. I imagine Long-Haired Dad, or more likely Heavy-Set Wife, eventually had enough and sent the large gypsy family on down the road toward Florida. Long-Haired Dad, minus Heavy-Set Wife and his own children, moved on to the greener pastures of Florida himself not long afterward.

The next family that moved in was a beautiful brunette woman and her three sons—the oldest of which was in my second grade class at school. His name was John. There was a younger brother named David and a toddler we all called Little Jim so he wouldn't be confused with Big Jim who lived across the street from us. The boys' mother was a divorcee. While that was not unheard of in the early 1970s, she was the first I had ever encountered. Apparently her husband had been wealthy and left her and the boys for another woman. They had moved to The Rental from a very large house and while their mother had to work all day now, they were able to retain their African American nanny from their previous life. She didn't live with them however. Every weekday morning and evening, she rode the bus that took her from "her people's" part of town to the Lion gas station and back again. She wore a white uniform and made the most beautiful peanut butter and jelly sandwiches. They were cut into perfect triangles with just the right ratio of apple jelly to peanut butter. She was always reading an old brown leather bible and could quote more of it by memory than anyone I had ever known before or since. She welcomed and fed me like I lived there. Those boys loved her and it was obvious she loved them having known them for better or worse, for richer or for poorer.

One day, I asked John why he didn't have a dad. He replied that the last time he had seen his father, he had stepped between his father's raised fist and his mother's face. His father had then picked up a nearby lamp and hurled it with such force across the room that it shattered in a hundred pieces against the opposite wall. When John told me this, I kept picturing it happening there in The Rental's tiny living room. It was only later I realized that this deathbed scene of his family's life was played out in a much larger room of a much larger house with a much fancier lamp.

They eventually moved on—hopefully to a real dad and more faithful husband. That is when the Hunters moved in. The Hunters had four children. The oldest was a sweet, responsible teenage girl named Terri. Then there were two boys named Gary and Woody. The youngest was a little blond haired girl—ironically also a manipulative crybaby like the preacher's daughter—named Tammie. The Hunters were living in the rental because they were building their own house somewhere way out in the country. The dad was very dark—dark hair, dark skin, dark countenance. He worked in some sort of roofer job during the week and every night and weekend he worked on his own house so I hardly ever saw him. Their mom worked at a local TV station full time so mostly it was teenage Terri who took care of The Rental house and her siblings. I think the

Hunters were there only a couple of years but they must have been important years because it seemed so much longer. This was the time in history right before cable TV and video games and VCRs and computers. Although we didn't know it at the time, it was really the dying breath, the sunset, the curtain call—all those overused euphemisms –of the fresh air freedom of an outdoor American childhood. We were truly the last generation that spent morning until night –even in the sweltering sauna of gulf coast summers—not in our air conditioned houses in front of screens, but on our bikes, on our carports, in the vacant lots and backyards, in the woods and beside the creeks and drainage ditches. Those are my memories of my time with the Hunter children—especially the boys. Gary, on whom I had a pre-teen crush, was definitely the nicer of the two. Woody was in a word—wild. On the first day they moved in The Rental, it was a hot and humid Mobile day and we all bought ice cream from the truck that sang though our neighborhood every afternoon. Woody had some kind of chocolate covered Eskimo bar. It melted as he was about half way through and it fell off the stick onto their grease-stained dirty carport. He promptly got down on his hands and knees and licked every bit of it up like a puppy. I just stared unbelieving. Gary looked at me knowingly and said "Its okay--Woody's a little crazy." Yeah. Thus began my crush on Gary and my watchfulness of Woody. The kind of awareness one would feel around a wild animal kept at home as a pet or someone that was mentally unstable in a hospital—the sense that although you were seemingly in a safe place, you were always on your guard. That if the hairs began to stand up on the back of your neck, the predator was loose and you needed to "run like hell" as my WWII veteran uncle would say. He occasionally pulled and yanked at his chain but the wild animal in Woody never completely broke free –at least while they lived next door. And Gary was always there to defend and protect me from him anyway. Gary always treated me like a friend and not just a girl. We made forts in the woods and played lots of football and kickball in the vacant lot. We jumped the red dirt hills at the end of the pavement with our bikes. We crawled on our hands and knees with our homemade backpacks playing army in the tall grass in the field behind our houses. We climbed trees. We played house and jail. We sat out in the gutter past dark talking about whatever 11 year old kids talk about.

They moved away very suddenly and I remember feeling so sad and lost for weeks afterward. I kept asking my parents, "How can they live in their new house? Its not even finished!" They responded that they had worked so hard on it for years and complete or not, it was livable and they were ready to go. I imagined them all sleeping on the plywood floors with the exposed pipes and electrical wires –but with the pride of a sturdy and well-constructed roof- and part of me wanted to move in with them. Years later, I ran into Gary Hunter at a local Pizza Hut. I remember having on a strapless dress and just coming back from the beach with a tan. I watched his jaw literally drop when he saw me. I wasn't a gangly, shy eleven year old anymore. Neither the girl he was with, who he introduced as his fiancé, nor my boyfriend next to me, seemed near as happy to be acquainted with us as Gary and I were to be re-united with each other—even if it was only for a minute.

My little family of three finally moved on to a larger house when I was about thirteen. I spent my teenage years with a two car garage—not a carport—and enough distance between our neighbors that an explosion could have happened and we may not have noticed. My parents kept ownership of our little brown house and rented it out. The neighborhood changed as most neighborhoods do. It became more diverse, less family-friendly, a little more "sketchy." Not long after we moved, a man and his wife bought The Rental and set up a business building wooden pallets in the backyard. Having a backyard business in the city limits may not have been entirely legal so just to make sure he wasn't openly breaking the law, he put up an 8 foot privacy fence around the perimeter of his whole back property including the little strip of yard between his carport at The Former Rental and our little carport at The Current Rental. No curious, intuitive children could peek into the daily dramas of their neighbors anymore. After scores of their own renters through the years, my parents finally sold their old little house. It is now known as a government "Section 8" home and last I heard, a single mom with seven children lives there. As far as I know, although his wife passed away, the "pallet" man still lives next door—thirty four years later—and still builds pallets. Or at least I hope that's what he's doing behind that fence. I also hope at least one of those seven children that live next door isn't too engrossed in her video games and smartphone to check if there just might be a three ring circus, complete with an occasional creepy clown and wild animal, living just beyond her carport-- a slight distance away and hidden from adult sight. She really should climb up and take a look.

ᴄᴙ

Mary Ann Wyatt is the Co-founder and Managing Editor for Wyatt House Publishing. She also works with her husband, Mark, on many of their books' interior layouts and cover designs. She has a BA in English/Creative Writing from the University of South Alabama and former work experience in magazine editing, public relations, advertising, layout and writing for corporate publications. Since the birth of their first child, Mary Ann has been a stay at home Mom and has helped Mark lead churches in Fort Worth, Texas; Flower Mound, Texas and for the last ten years, Deeper Life Fellowship in Mobile, Alabama—her native city. She and Mark have four wonderful children—Samuel, 20, Sarah, 18, Nathaniel, 15, and Autumn, 10.

A Storied Life

by Kenny Thacker

We all carry a story. It's imbedded deeply into our souls. It commands our lives as surely as our DNA code determines the color of our eyes. It was put there by God.

I grew up in the mountains of southeastern Kentucky. My great great's left the British Isles to slowly find their way to the head of a little creek called Troublesome. They put down deep roots. They lived off the land for many years until coal deposits were discovered in their beloved hills. It was then they began to live off what was under the land. Most all of the men in my family line have dug coal from underneath a hillside. It was hard living, some would say it was not living at all, merely an existence, but I disagree. I grew up well.

Some of my fondest memories are sitting on the front

porch listening to my grandpa tell stories. He told all kinds of stories. Funny stories, sad stories, stories of local characters, but all stories of hard work and hard living colored with redeeming values. He passed his life into me through his story. One of my favorite things to do now is to tell stories to my grandchildren. I think of him often while I'm doing it.

I thought there was no other story that could shape my life more than my grandpa's. But that was before I heard the gospel.

I was introduced to Jesus when I was in my late teens. I didn't know very much about Him at all, but I was certain my life had totally changed. All my plans had been disrupted and I discovered I was pretty happy about it. The one thing I was sure of is that I wanted to know Him more. I wanted to know His story. I had no idea I was beginning a lifelong journey.

Tony was there when I came to faith. He was a true friend, a real companion in Christ. He walked the walk. He was instrumental in my life in so many ways when I first met the Lord. I'll never forget one day in particular that would prove to change my life forever. After one more of our all too frequent late night fellowship/prayer/bible study/ goofin' off sessions, we wound up spending the night at his grandma's house. The next morning it happened. He came into the room where I had slept and threw a big, black bible down on the bed. "Here man, I believe God wants me to give you this." It was a New American Standard version. I couldn't put it down. He had given me a copy of the story. It has shaped my life. I still have and use that bible. It has a special place in my office, but more so in my soul. It was because of getting that Bible into my hands that God would begin to get His story into my head and into my heart. That was over thirty years ago, and now I think I'm starting to get it.

I never had a great relationship with my earthly father. He was a hard working man and provided for us very well. He gave us things, but didn't give us himself. He was a fairly angry guy. He had his own reasons for being angry that I would come to understand years later, but we missed out on the kind of relationship God intended for a father and son to have. It would be a long time before I would discover how much that contributed to my frustration with this gift Tony had given me.

I started reading this book where you start reading any book, the beginning. When I found out that God was a father that was not good news to me. I cautiously read about this great God, this ultimate Father, who walked and talked with his children in the cool of the day in this incredible place called Paradise. They worked together as Father and son. They enjoyed each other's company. This seemed so different to me, almost too good to be true. Then, not very far into the story at all, it happened.

God had told Adam and Eve that they had the run of the garden. He wanted them to enjoy it, work it and savor its fruit. There was just one rule. There were two trees in the garden; the tree of life and the tree of the knowledge of good and evil. The one rule was to not eat of the tree of the knowledge of good and evil. We all know that if you give a human being one rule, he's going to break it. They broke it. They ate of the tree. It's important to note that before they ate of the tree of the knowledge of good and evil, they had no knowledge of good and evil. This means they had no concept of "being good" or "being bad", they only had a concept of being with God.

When God "found out" that they had eaten of the tree He came looking for them. They were hiding behind a bush, afraid of a God who had never given them any reason to think He was even capable of anger. My heart began to race reading this. What will God do now that His kids have messed up? I was afraid I knew what was going to happen. I was right.

God dealt with their mistake instantly and severely. He forcibly evicted them from the garden. Of course he did, that's how father are. I knew it was too good to be true. He's now revealing what He's really like. If you make one mistake, you're kicked out. Adam and Eve lost the right to live in sweet communion with Him in the garden and were banished from His presence. I had suspected as much. In that moment I developed a wrong idea about the nature of God that would stay with me a long time. I wish I had known that God kicked them out of the garden to keep them from getting to the tree of life. If they had eaten from it in the condition of separation they were in it would have been permanently sealed. There would have been no hope for restoration. God so loved them that he kept them from ultimate separation. The fact that he kept them away from the tree of life made reconciliation possible. I didn't know He was setting the stage for the hero of the story.

There are thousands of things that I know now that I wish I'd known then. We all have our lists. I wish I had known the true nature of God. Another one of the things I wish I had known is that the Bible is one big story about God's plan to display and actuate His nature into us through Jesus. For many years I used it faithfully, but not well. I somehow managed to make it about me. I had mistakenly believed the bible was an owner's manual for life. I looked for rules to keep, and I found them by the dozen. The problem was I couldn't keep all of them no matter how hard I tried. Approaching the Bible as rulebook created a deep frustration inside me. I knew in my spirit this was a book of life, but it didn't seem to be producing much life in me. I knew I couldn't live up to its commands. I saw others who I assumed were being successful, but I just couldn't seem to wrangle my heart into obedience. Oh, I was able to get a handle on the "big sins". I didn't drink or smoke or chase girls or listen to rock and roll. I would think I was doing well, only to have a bad thought, or discover a terrible attitude. The rulebook kept pointing out my failure and I learned to "act like" everything was ok in my life. I had discovered religion and it ate away at my relationship with Jesus. I could never be good enough or obey long enough without messing up. I was a disappointment to myself and to God. Isaiah and Jeremiah reminded me often. I wasn't liking this story as much as I had imagined I would.

Then one day I heard the voice of God as clearly as I've ever heard it. He told me He was going to send fathers into my life. Thinking I knew the nature of fathers, that was not good news. I had no idea it was some of the best news I'd ever get.

One by one over the next five years God arranged for my path not just to cross, but also to join with these fathers. Primarily, it has been these men that have helped me get the story of the gospel straight. Their words and actions would prove to teach me about the true nature of a father and the true nature of the story of God. They changed my life forever and continue to do so. I continue to learn from them the true story of the gospel. As my perception of fathers changed I noticed that I felt more comfortable with God Himself. I realized I had been mistaken for many years about both Him and His story.

It seems so simple to say that the Bible is about Jesus and not me; yet that's the truth that rocked my world and changed the course of my life and ministry. I have come to learn that in the Bible, it's the big story of Jesus that gives all the smaller stories meaning and purpose. That same big, over-arching story allows our stories to make sense as well. Knowing that everything is ultimately about Him creates both reference and anchor points for every situation and circumstance we might encounter. We must approach the Bible as being about Him. It's not an owner's manual or a moral code; it's the story of the Savior. We'll never get the full benefits of having God's Word in print until we open it looking for Him.

In the mid 1800's, Gustav Freytag, a German novelist and playwright, developed a five part model for story. It was a framework that would help you understand the plot structure and better follow a story or play. The five parts are the Exposition, the Rising Action, the Climax, the falling Action and the Resolution. This model has helped me better understand the Gospel.

The exposition is the part of the story that creates the setting, introduces the characters, reveals where the story is going and also introduces some sort of conflict that alters the path of the story and threatens to change it altogether. In the bible this happens in the first few chapters of Genesis.

We meet the main character in the first verse. We'll find out a whole lot more about Him as the story progresses, but this lets us know the story is about Him. The setting begins to be developed. The heavens and the earth are mentioned, but our attention is immediately drawn to the earth, as if a stage is being set.

With sky, trees and vegetation for the backdrop, the stage is lit as God says, "Let there be light." Then are added a cast of innumerable extras. Enter swarms of living creatures flying in the sky, swimming in the sea and moving about on the earth. And then special attention is drawn to the creation of another character. This one is obviously not just an extra. It's a character who resembles God, but yet isn't. He's made in his image. Then God breathes life into him and he lives!! There would have been a crescendo in the score at that point.

Life rocks along as the intention of the story is revealed. The new character, Adam, is to live and work with God. His assignment is to fellowship and co labor with Him; to enjoy him as much as he enjoys himself. But then we hear a minor chord. The conflict is about to be introduced. Enter the snake. He tempts. Man sins. Paradise is lost. The conflict is that man has been separated from God with no hope of restoration.

Next comes the Rising Action. The role of the rising action is to describe how the story continues in the conflict that was created in the exposition. This section of the bible story will describe many attempts at correcting the conflict, but we'll soon find that none of them would succeed permanently. The rising action part of the story is covered from Genesis 4 all the way through Malachi.

Following the Rising Action comes what the whole world has been waiting on, the Climax. In the climax the main character makes a move that reveals a decision he has made that will correct and determine the outcome of the story. In the bible story the climax is Jesus. The hero has finally appeared! The conception, birth, life, suffering, death, burial, resurrection and ascension of Jesus IS the climax of history. The arrival of Jesus will prove to change everything permanently. This will prove to solve the problem of separation from God. The Bible covers the climax of God's big story at the beginning of the New Testament in Matthew right on through and up into Acts chapter 2.

The greatest event that has ever happened, or that will ever happen, has happened; the Christ event. Emmanuel, God with us. This changes everything. There is now a new way to relate to God. New protocol has been introduced instructing us in how to relate to Him. In other words, there is a new contract that requires new instruction. The old way of relating to God is over, it's obsolete. The old covenant has been fulfilled and now we're being introduced to the new one. In the story, this is where we move from the OT into the NT. Do you think it will be difficult for people who for generation after generation related to God under the old way to learn to live in the new way? It will take time and solid, consistent teaching.

This moves us into the part of the story called the Falling Action. This is where the hero has done something to change the story and adjustments have to be made to life because of his action. We can expect some turbulence. Life has changed. Those of you who are married will know that once you enter into the marriage contract, life changes. If because of great love for your spouse you honor the contract it can be a joyful deal. However, if you keep living like you were when you were on your own, you can expect turbulence and not a whole lot of joy. So, once we've settled the fact of God's love, we can expect plenty of awkwardness and surprises as we learn the new way to relate to God, but rest in our restoration as we go.

The bible covers the falling action of the story from Acts 2 well into the book of Revelation. Actually, we are still in the falling action on our place in the storyline. We are better learning how to approach life in the context of the big story of the gospel. We are still learning how to apply what Jesus has done to every aspect of our lives.

The last chapters of the book of Revelation give us the clearest picture of the final purposes of God and describe the Resolution. We see the "old" heaven and earth give way to new dominion, which is ruled totally and completely by the Lord. John saw the New Jerusalem coming down;

don't miss that. The new is being imposed on the old. Remember what the loud voice from the throne says; "Now the dwelling place of God is with men, and He will live with them. They will be His people, and God Himself will be with them and be their God." - Rev 21:3

We see a new earth with no death, sickness or pain. Harmony and unity have been totally restored with God. We have been restored to living in the community of the Trinity. We discover that renewed creation has been the goal all along.

Nothing is going to happen in the future that will trump what has already happened at the cross. It's important to remember that Jesus was the climax of the story. The resolution is a summation of what has happened and what will be fulfilled and brought to ultimate resolution because of the action of the hero.

Understanding the story of Jesus is the only thing that brings the daily peace, wisdom, joy and transformation that we so desperately need. I am different because of hearing His story.

I realize today what a blessed man I am. I'm surrounded not only by a family that loves me, but also joined to a spiritual family of fathers, mothers, brothers, sisters, sons and daughters that God has graciously allowed me to do life with. They all have a part in revealing and actuating the gospel in my life. Obviously, the "too good to be true" still continues to be a vibrant, restorative, joyful relationship with the Father, Son and Holy Spirit. I have found my place in the story. I'd love to sit with you on the front porch and tell it to you sometime.

☙

Kenny Thacker is a musically gifted minister who carries a unique anointing for prophetic insight impacting today's church, as well as a heart for true discipleship. His rare sense of humor opens hearts to receive the Word of God. Kenny's passion is assisting people in discovering who they are in Christ, developing their gifts, and seeing them released into God's purpose for their lives. He has been active in ministry for over 25 years as a Pastor, Worship Leader and popular national/international conference speaker.

Originally from Kentucky, he and his beautiful wife, Lynn, now reside in Prosper, Texas where he serves as President and Founder of SoundWord, Inc. and on the Leadership Team of the Kerygma Network of Churches.

A Picture

by Emily LaForce

Mama sat sewing in her wooden rocking chair when her six-year-old daughter, Victoria, came in and asked,

"Mama, why has Uncle Eric been in the library so long? Is he sick?"

"Yes, dear."

"What does he have?"

Mama sighed, "He's sick with heart break."

"What's that?" Victoria asked curiously.

"It's when you're really sad. He misses Rose and Joseph."

Victoria nodded and teared up.

Mama noticed and asked," What's wrong dear?"

"I miss Rose too. And I never even met Joseph! I think I have heart break too..."

Mama chuckled and said, "Uncle Eric will get better. He just needs peace, quiet, and time to think. So that means you can't play with him until he feels better."

Victoria frowned and asked, "Wouldn't I make him feel better? When I play, it makes me feel better."

"It's different with heart break. Just give him some time."

Victoria sighed and acquiesced.

Suddenly, Victoria had an idea and ran off to her room. She would make her Uncle Eric feel better if she could help it.

Mama rolled her eyes and went back to her sewing, wondering what her daughter was up to now.

Heart break did have strange effects on people, particularly Eric Welsh. He hardly ate anything in the past month because he lacked the appetite, rarely left the library and often sat in an uncomfortable, wooden chair, vacantly staring out the window.

The main reason why he kept a daily vigil at the window was because he was looking for a glimpse of his former life. His brother's house was in a good neighborhood with many young families and so Eric looked for what he had lost. Suddenly, a young woman walked by the window, pushing a buggy with a gurgling babe inside.

Although this was what he had been searching for, it pulled at his heart and he was transported to two years earlier.

He'd just married Rose, her dark hair pulled back behind her wedding veil. She said she would love him forever and he marveled at how he had gotten someone as wonderful as her.

Then, he remembered how she looked ten months ago when the doctor told them they were pregnant. Her face glowed as tears of joy slipped down her cheeks. He started to dream of having a boy. The boy would be named Joseph, after Eric's father.

Then, he remembered that horrible night filled with Rose's screams and finally, a blank silence. One could faintly hear the pitiful cooing of a baby. An hour later, the cooing ceased.

Now Eric didn't have a family anymore because his parents had already passed on.

The continual question that ran through his mind was why.

Why would God allow this to happen? Didn't he want the best for his life and continually work for his good?

Father Michael's proclamations of the goodness of God echoed in Eric's mind, but he couldn't see how it could be true because of what happened.

Most of all, he missed Rose. He recalled their days of courtship and their short marriage of two years with nostalgia. He only wished he could erase the image of Rose's pale, cold face from his mind.

Lost in reflection, he didn't notice the door of the library quietly open and the soft step of Victoria approach him.

When he finally noticed her, he jumped and asked, "What are you doing here?"

With a hurt look in her eyes, "Do you not want me here?"

He smiled, "Yes, I want you here. You just startled me is all."

Suddenly, a thought occurred to her and she said, "We have to be quiet so Mama won't hear us."

Eric grinned slightly and asked, "And why might that be?"

Victoria replied matter of factly, "Because she thinks I'm taking a nap and I can't talk to you until you feel better."

And then another thought occurred to her and she asked, "Are you feeling better yet?"

Eric chuckled and lied to appease the little girl, "A little."

"Well, I made you a picture to make you feel all better."

And she pulled a folded piece of paper out of her dress pocket and handed it to Eric.

He unfolded it and then tears tracked down his face.

Unaware of Eric's tears, Victoria explained the picture, "This is Aunt Rose," she pointed to a woman with wings and a smile of joy on her face, "And this is Joseph," she pointed to a giggling baby with wings.

"And that's Jesus in the middle," she pointed to a man with rays of light radiating from his whole face. Jesus gazed lovingly at Rose and Joseph, and the sight pricked Eric's heart.

Victoria looked at his face for approval and found tears coming down his face.

She touched his face, wiping his tears away and asked, "Why are you crying? Did it make you sad?"

"No…it made me happy…Sometimes people cry…because they're happy."

Eric felt peace wash over him as he actually saw his wife's smiling face with Jesus and his son. Although he still grieved their deaths, he knew that he would see them again. Surely if his family was at peace, God was still good.

"Good. Do you want to play?"

Eric wiped his face, a grin forming and then replied, "That would be great."

☙

Emily La Force is a native of Mobile, Alabama attending the University of Mobile in pursuit of a music composition degree with a minor in English. Her work has been published in The Foxhole Report, University of Mobile's weekly newsletter. Reading and writing have always been a great passion for her and she has a strong call on her life to glorify God through writing whether it be in short stories, devotionals, or even novels. She hopes to inspire others and point them to Christ through her stories. She is currently writing her first novel. You can reach Emily on Facebook, theforce24.tumblr.com, or you can email her at emilylaforce2@gmail.com.

LIFE LESSONS FROM THE ROAD

by Jamie Harvill

My earliest experience in performing was playing guitar and singing in church plays and school talent shows. In my teens I even made a few bucks playing in dance bands with names like Arabesque and Dark Star. When I became a Christian, I played with groups like Homeward Bound, and Luke Luker and the New Life Gospel Singers. Although we spent more time practicing in someone's garage than playing gigs, the experience I gained helped build a foundation that would prepare me for the fateful phone call I would receive in early 1980.

American Entertainment Productions was a small company situated in the northern suburbs of Columbus, Ohio. It might have been a tiny blip on the radar-screen of the entertainment industry, but it has been a "performance school" for many college-aged musicians and singers since 1973.

Wes Turner, the company's talent coordinator, had received a recommendation that I audition as a guitar player for one of their touring groups. At the time of the call I was making plans to take a job driving a school bus, after poor grades discouraged me from continuing on to my second year of college. Needless to say, I was intrigued with the offer. Wes Turner was very convincing, too. He said that the group would be playing Top-40 music for junior and senior high school assemblies, and that we'd also be playing show music (think Up With People) for corporate conventions in the evenings. Additionally, there was an upcoming USO tour to Germany and Iceland on the books for the spring. What bored and frustrated 19-year-old would balk at that?

Though extremely excited, I was also filled with anxiety, thinking about leaving home for the first time, setting off in a van full of strangers, and traveling to places I had only heard about in history books and geography class. I was a homebody, but I was also a dreamer, and I couldn't turn down this extraordinary offer. After passing the audition, I bought my plane ticket, shopped for new clothes, and headed off into the wild blue yonder.

Wes called me on a Friday morning and, like a whirlwind, by that Sunday night, I was standing in the baggage claim of the Toledo Airport, waiting for the group to pick me up. When I stepped onto that van as the newest member of the group *Life*, my life changed forever.

For the next three years I learned how to be an entertainer— an MC and a front person in a group. I learned the discipline of pretending that I was having a blast on stage; one time while sick with a 103-degree fever. I learned how to sleep for 8 hours-straight while sitting upright in a cramped van. I studied the art and skill of capturing, keeping and bringing joy to an audience, in any setting, indoors or out—rain or shine.

My tenure with American Entertainment Productions (AEP) took me all over the North America and the world, and I played for a U.S. Presidents, politicians, Fortune 500 CEOs, opened for world-famous singers and comedians in Vegas casinos and big-city theaters, spent a summer playing in Disney World, made the county fair circuit across Canada, and carried gear over garbage-filled loading docks, through slippery kitchens, into hotel ballrooms—way too many to count. By the time January of 1983 rolled around, I was a seasoned performer, and eventually an experienced road manager who could deal with promoters, get a band to every gig on time, and faithfully practiced the motto: "The show must go on!"

I became a world-traveler; my world became bigger in the process.

I consider the AEP experience to be my "secular" training, but God also had another opportunity for me that would prove to be my "sacred" training. In January of 1983, I received a call from Greg Golden in Mobile, Alabama.

The invitation from Greg to audition subsequently led to a 2-1/2-year stint with the group Truth. The group's founder and leader was a gentleman named Roger Breland. He was sensitive to his listeners and had an incredible gift for weaving funny stories and tender spiritual moments together. He would turn around, with his back to the audience, to conduct the band and singers. He has always delivered. Roger Breland is a true entertainer.

Truth--in the span of 30 years--and before Roger retired the group in 2001--did almost 10,000 concerts, recorded 50 albums, traveled to more than two dozen countries, and has performed to a combined audience of more than 10 million people. Truth's success was based largely on Roger (Mr. B as we called him) and his ability to recognize a great "moment."

I observed how Roger eased audiences into the palm of his hand every night during my tenure with Truth. I am still using some of those techniques I learned way back in 1983-85. I gleaned invaluable experience playing to secular audiences while traveling with AEP, too. These performance and ministry "schools" were a benefit to me, even today, as I plan and prepare worship services. An effective worship service contains much of the same ingredients and techniques as a secular performance. The biggest exception in worship is that the congregation becomes the lead singer and God is the audience!

These days I like to stay close to home. If I'm asked to perform or participate in a conference, my honorarium is really for the travel--since playing, singing and speaking is a treat. Essentially, I get paid to leave home. The person I am today is a product of my experiences on the road. I learned much about human nature, who to trust and of whom to be leery. I learned to value home, mostly by not having one for six years, save the small band of musicians with which I lived. Dorothy Gale got it right when she said, "There's no place like home!" This is probably my greatest lesson learned from the road.

⟨⟩

Jamie is a native of Southern California and grew up in the shadow of Disney, Fender guitars, Hollywood and the Pacific Ocean. He is best known for writing worship songs such as Ancient of Days, Firm Foundation, Because We Believe, and Garments of Praise. His world-travels as a musician and conference teacher allowed him to minister throughout Asia, Europe, the Mediterranean, and all of North America, He now lives near Nashville, TN, where he continues to write songs, author books and articles, teach seminars on worship, record new music, and lead the worship band at a wonderful church. He's been married to Brenda since 1985. Both of their children are happily married. Jamie and Brenda recently welcomed their first grandchild in September, 2012.

Revealing Responses

by Monica Warren

Approximately three and a half months before His crucifixion, Jesus brings a dead man, Lazarus, back to life. As the events unfold, John provides his reader with the responses of those caught up in the drama. By looking at the story through the lenses of their responses, we almost certainly will discover something about ourselves and those around us. It is my hope and prayer for each of us that these discoveries will further empower us to live the abundant life that Jesus promises and more effectively advance His Kingdom on this earth.

Jesus & His Disciples

The story, found in the Gospel of John chapter 11, begins something like this...

Jesus, while with His disciples some distance away up the Jordan River, receives word that a beloved friend, Lazarus, is gravely ill. Rather than leave immediately to make the 20 mile journey to Bethany where Lazarus and his sisters – Mary and Martha – live, Jesus waits two days before departing. During this time, He informs the disciples that Lazarus' sickness will not lead to death but to the glory of God. When Jesus finally announces travel plans to Bethany, the disciples attempt to persuade Him otherwise. After all, the last visit to Jerusalem (only two short miles from Bethany) included an attempt to execute Jesus with stones! Despite this, after a misunderstood inference to Lazarus napping, Jesus bluntly tells the disciples that Lazarus is dead, and they are going to him. As Jesus nears Bethany, He and His entourage learn that Lazarus died four days ago.

(Side note: John does not tell his readers the number of days since Lazarus' death simply to mark the time of Jesus' delay in coming. Jews held the belief that, after death, the departed's spirit hovered around the tomb seeking reentry into the body. However, after four days, believing the face had decayed and was no longer recognizable, the person's spirit would leave. In other words, Lazarus is REALLY DEAD.)

In the opening scene, John provides the only mention of the disciples in the entire story. Their responses to situation at hand reveal that their focus is on the physical and temporal. However, Jesus offers them a glimpse of the spiritual and eternal – a greater reality and a grander purpose – God's glory (see John 11:4). In light of this, we might ask ourselves, when we look at circumstances – both our personal situations and the things happening on the larger stage of humanity – do we look through the lens of the physical and temporal? Or do we look through the lens of the spiritual and eternal? Rest assured, our perspective will determine our response. A physical/temporal focus drives us to live holding onto this life and all it offers, as if this is all there is. So, when life takes an unpleasant turn, we writhe and wrestle and worry, white knuckling anything we can, or think we can, control. Conversely, with eyes fixed on the spiritual and eternal, we live like something better awaits us. After all, those who love and follow Jesus possess a glorious future, one in which the best anything pales in comparison. Adopting this latter perspective, when life takes an unpleasant turn, we may writhe and wrestle, but ultimately we rest ourselves in the hands of a sovereign God, who works out all things for our good and His glory.

Jesus & Mary and Martha

Leaving Jesus and the disciples where John does, on the road to Bethany, we enter the home of Martha and Mary...

Can you see her? Martha? Her body has gone into autopilot. She straightens the house and makes preparations in an attempt to order the external hoping that it will somehow calm the fierce internal storm of grief. Then, with the announcement for which she had been waiting for days—but had not come—Martha drops what she has been doing and rushes out the door, down the road to meet Jesus. When she reaches Him, Martha pours out accusations in one breath, "If you had been here..." And expresses her faith in the next, "...anything you ask of God will be done." After a brief and perplexing exchange about life and death and resurrection, now and later, Martha returns home to fetch Mary.

Grief's presence is palpable as Martha nears the house. She presses past the crowd and finds Mary where she left her, sitting against the wall, lost in her pain. Gently, Martha cups her sister's cheek in her hand and bends over, whispering in Mary's ear, "Rabboni nears; He calls for you." Immediately, Mary brings her hand to her lips. Tears begin to fall as she runs out the door. She does not notice the crowd following her. She does not notice that her lungs are screaming for oxygen as she runs, sobbing, toward the figure of a man she recognizes as Jesus standing in the distance. As Mary's legs carry her toward Him, her mind races with questions, accusations, and what-ifs. She reaches Jesus, her knees crumble, and her emotions explode into words as she cries out, "Lord, if only You had been here, my brother would still be alive."

Before we glean from Martha and Mary's responses, we need to look at one more exchange between Jesus and Martha which comes a little later in our story. When Jesus orders the stone rolled away from the tomb, Martha verbalizes what everyone thinks, "By now, Lazarus stinks!"

Now, looking at every response from Mary and Martha recorded by John, what can we see? While they loved Jesus and clearly believed His identity and power and authority, they had limited Him. Can you hear it? "If only You had been here..." In other words, "You COULD have saved our brother, but it is too late. He is dead. You possess the power and authority to save from death. But now, Lazarus is beyond hope, beyond Your scope of power and authority. " So, we hold the mirror up to our own lives and ponder, in what ways do we limit Jesus? In what circumstances or relationships have we decided that Jesus needed to have intervened before this or that? Asserting that, at the point, the situation remains beyond Jesus' reach, beyond repair, beyond redemption.

When all seems lost, when things have not turned out as we had hoped, had thought best, or had even remotely understood, two choices lie before us. Will we abandon hope by limiting Jesus? Or will we boast that nothing is impossible with our God? Please hear my heart. I am NOT suggesting denial, shallow clichés, or any sort of Name-it-Claim-it Prosperity Gospel. Remember, it is not the quantity of our faith but the object onto which we place our faith. And our faith lies in a God who can, and will, raise the dead – physical, mental, spiritual, emotional – to LIFE! In this world wracked with sin, painful and tragic things happen. So grieve but do not despair. Mourn but against the backdrop of hope. Weep and wail but mingle songs of victory amidst your sobs. Finally, suffer with an eye on redemption. For REDEMPTION HAS COME AND IS COMING IN FULL!

Jesus & the Mourners

Continuing with the narrative...

> When Jesus sees everyone's grief, He is deeply moved and intensely troubled. Upon request, Jesus is taken to where Lazarus lies entombed within a small cave behind a massive stone. Jesus weeps. Watching Jesus, some decide He surely loved Lazarus. But skeptical others come to a different conclusion, i.e., if Jesus really loved Lazarus, He would have come sooner.

> Jesus fully engaged in this life. The events and

people in life deeply affected Him. And the community present at the tomb that day judged Jesus' heart and intention by His outward response to Lazarus' illness – specifically, Jesus' delay in coming. Turning the tables, we must ask ourselves, what do we use as the barometer of God's love and goodness toward us? Do we use the outward appearance of our circumstances? Or do we rely on the truth about the nature and character of God? Too many have embraced the lie that good things and prosperity are the indicator of God's love and goodness. This implies (if not straight-up spoken) that bad things and hardships are evidence of His disapproval with us. Instead of such a limited, Western perspective, take a look back at history – both of all creation and yours personally. See a God who has pursued us lovingly and relentlessly and unashamedly! Biblical love is the commitment to do God's best for another no matter what it costs the giver. And in the case of our God, it cost Him the life of His Son, Jesus. What greater love exists? How much more can our God do to prove His love and goodness toward us?

Raising Lazarus & the Aftermath

Now, to the climax and summation of the drama...

> All eyes are on Jesus. His voice breaks through the sounds of mourning, "Remove the stone." After Martha and Jesus have a brief exchange concerning the inevitable odor of one deceased and about seeing

the glory of God, the stone is rolled from its resting place. Jesus raises His eyes, and speaks so that the listening crowd can hear, "Lazarus, come forth!" A stunned crowd stands silent and motionless in disbelief at Jesus' audacious command. All eyes fix on the dark cavernous hole that personifies how death itself has swallowed their beloved Lazarus. Within moments, to everyone's complete shock and dismay, a figure, completely wrapped in burial clothes, emerges from the shadows. Shrieks and gasps fill the air. Could it really be Lazarus? Jesus orders the figure be unbound and released. This action reveals that Lazarus IS very much alive... back from the dead! Inexpressible joy fills the air that just moments ago had been held captive in the grip of death and mourning. Never had anyone brought someone BACK from the dead. True, prophets past had revived the dead, but to snatch a four-day-old corpse from the grave? Who is this Jesus?!

Jesus' actions demand a response.

As a result of Jesus raising Lazarus from the dead, many of the Jews believe Him to be who He says He is. However, others, confounded by what they have just witnessed, take their questions to the Pharisees. Will this turn of events shed light on the true identity of this man? Maybe He really is the long-awaited Messiah, the object of our hopes and dreams. Surely the religious leaders will know the truth. So, others go to them...with their questions.

John does not tell us how the disciples or even the trio of siblings respond to this inconceivably joyful turn of events. Although silent about our main characters, John does reveal how the community of eyewitnesses react. That is, many Jews believed in Jesus, but others reported the events to the Pharisees. Note that John does not tell us whether or not this second group believed, but simply that they reported the events to the Pharisees. The Pharisees were a sect of Jewish religious leaders and Jesus' primary opposition. Granted, this second group of witnesses to Lazarus' resurrection may very well have not believed and simply desired to tattle on Jesus. But, perhaps not...at least not all of them. What if, as I conjectured in the narrative, in reporting the events, this group of individuals was looking to the religious of their day – those who claimed to know God and His ways and follow Him – to give them an answer for the events swirling around them? Looking to them to ultimately answer the question, "Who is this Jesus?"

Do you remember what happened as a result of these eyewitness reports given to the Pharisees? According to the remainder of John chapter 11, the Jewish religious leaders called an emergency council meeting. At this meeting, they did not identify Jesus to be the long-awaited Messiah. Instead, they determined to kill Jesus.

My question here for you and me is this. What if the same thing happens today – albeit in more subtle ways? What if people are turning to us, the professing Christians – the religious of our day, who claim to know God and His ways and follow Him – to answer their questions? Might they be turning to us to help make sense of the unfolding events in their personal lives and the world around them? Ultimately, can they find answers to their questions about Jesus (God) and how He relates, if at all, to them? And if there is truth to this speculation, what are you and I communicating to them?

I suspect our answers to their spoken and unspoken questions are more indirect than we realize. It seems people care very little about doctrines and theologies and anything that even hints of hypocritical lip service. Instead, folks watch and listen to our responses in life's unfolding events to determine what we really believe about Jesus (God). They silently process these responses to determine: Is there a God? Is there really life after physical death, and if so, what kind of life? Is our God really worthy of their passion and pursuit? Is our God trustworthy and dependable? Is our God really strong enough to handle their life problems, pains, and hidden pasts? Is our God really good and loving – incapable of anything but His very best toward them?

Make no mistake, our responses to what life throws at us screams to a broken and hurting world what we really believe about life and Jesus. Reflecting on the aforementioned questions, may our answers always line up with Truth. As a result, may we live the abundant life that Jesus promises us and more effectively advance His Kingdom on this earth. Now, to Him who is the One Worthy Pursuit of this life be all glory and honor and praise in and through us!

Looking at life's trials as filtered through the hands of a loving God, Monica Warren has come to believe that "God is incapable of anything but His very best towards her." Out of the confidence of this truth, Monica lives her life, writes, and teaches God's Word to others with a contagious passion. After twelve years of faithfully leading women's ministry in her local church and serving on a teaching cadre for adult Sunday school, God is opening doors for Monica to bring His message of love, life, and hope through writing and teaching to a wider audience. Monica resides in Mobile, Alabama with her husband, Claude, where together they are discovering the joys of a new season as they release their two college-aged children, Benjamin and Sydney, into the plans and purposes God has for them.

A DANCE WITH ETERNAL IMPACT

by Lonnie Honeycutt

(Excerpted from *"Living Jesus Out Loud"*)

Those who volunteer with 99 for 1 Ministries are a very loving, extremely enthusiastic and diverse group of Christians who believe we're called to follow James 2:14-17 in a very literal manner. As the president and lead volunteer of 99 for 1 Ministries, a para-church ministry dedicated to serving the under-loved wherever we find them, I'm often called upon to go places and do things most Christians are never faced with. More often than I can easily count I've been called upon to help prostitutes, drug-users, alcoholics, those who are homeless and those on the verge or in the midst of an attempted suicide. The type of ministry God has given us is one that does not always allow us to immediately know the impact He has had on those to whom we're sent to minister. Frequently we receive reports well after the fact of how those we've ministered to have been blessed. Thankfully, this isn't always the case.

One story I've been able to tell and retell, much to my listeners and readers delight, took place just before Thanksgiving a couple of years ago. While I've changed the names, all the details are accurate. With this being said, let me tell you a story...

Very recently I was asked to bring some clothes for a little girl (7 years old) whose family was having a difficult time – one of the families we're trying to gather Christmas money for. I had no information other than that her name was Lindsey, her dress size was a 7 and that she wanted either sleeveless or short sleeves dresses and/or shirts. I was also told she liked clothes that 'poofed-out' when she spun around. I was assured that even if I couldn't find short-sleeved shirts her mom could hem them.

Armed with only that information I went to our storage shed (which is bursting with clothes for children thanks to the donations from people who have given generously to 99 for 1 Ministries). Admittedly, I struggled to find clothes for a little girl with whom I'd never had contact (I didn't know her favorite color or how tall she was or the 'type' of material she'd really like – factors which I'm highly aware are very important to girls because I have an 8 year old daughter myself). In any case, in about two hours, I was able to find about a half dozen dresses, about the same amount of pants and a nice, warm coat.

It took me over an hour and a half to find Lindsey's home (a trailer that's kind of out in the boonies). When I drove up I was immediately greeted by 3 dogs (big dogs – the kind we have at our house), all of which were barking and growling and wagging their tails at the same time. Not being exceptionally brave – especially when it comes to animals that can take chunks out of me – I decided to call the family phone from the safety of my truck.

As luck would have it, their phone was busy. I tried redialing and even honking my horn a couple of times (which stirred the dogs up into a slobbering frenzy) but no one came to the door. After about 10 minutes I was annoyed. Annoyed to the point I thought about just leaving and having the family meet me somewhere that was more territorially friendly (such as anywhere their three dogs wouldn't be able to size me up as a snack food).

Just as I was about to put my truck into reverse I saw movement from inside the trailer. The curtains parted a bit and I saw a little girls face beaming from within. She quickly disappeared. Then, a few seconds later, her little face popped back into view and I could tell she was calling out to someone inside the trailer.

Soon enough a woman came to the door, called her dogs

inside and yelled for me to wait just a few minutes while she put them in their crates. I was more than happy to do so.

A couple of minutes later the mother walked out of her front door, came to my truck and invited me inside. I grabbed the plastic bags I'd brought Lindsey's clothes in and, as I walked towards the door of their home, I heard Lindsey excitedly ask, "Dad, is that the white pastor who is bringing me the dresses?"

Though I didn't hear her father's response I knew he'd affirmed that he thought I was because I heard the squeal of delight that only a little girl can make (the kind that's so shrill it can only be matched in decibels by the wail of a siren).

As soon as I walked into the door I was greeted by a man in a wheelchair whose hair was still dripping wet. It turned out his wife had been in the bathroom helping him get out of the bathtub when I first arrived which hindered them from coming out to meet me – and it also explained the short ramp his wife and I had just walked up. Darlene and George are huggers, just like me, so I immediately felt at ease. But, Lindsey wasn't anywhere around.

After explaining to me that Lindsey was extremely shy around strangers Darlene went to collect her daughter. George and I talked while I laid the clothes I'd brought his daughter on their couch. Several minutes later Darlene appeared with Lindsey peeking out from behind her as they walked towards me.

"Hi," I said. "I didn't know what kind of dresses you liked so I picked the ones I thought my own daughter would like."

When Lindsey finally spied all of the clothes that were behind me (I'd knelt down to her level) her eyes came to life and, without warning, she ran to me to give me a hug.

Folks, I've got to tell you, I can't remember ever feeling as awkward as I did in that moment.

Lindsey ran to me so quickly that I wrapped my arms around her before I realized that she had no arms. Instead, she laid her face against my neck and kind of snuggled with me.

The hug was over in a moment and she asked Darlene, "Mommy, can I try this one on?"

Lindsey had chosen the brightest, most multi-colored dress in the bunch (my daughter calls them gypsy dresses because of a play she was in once). George told Lindsey she could try them on after I left because he was certain I had a lot of other business to take care of. As just about any seven year old who is excited would do, Lindsey pleaded and, after I said I could spare a few minutes, her parents capitulated and the little girl picked the dress up in her lips and ran towards her bedroom – her mother following behind.

After being sincerely thanked by George and offered a cold drink, he and I began to talk. To make a long story short, here's a synopsis of what I found out while Lindsey was changing into her new clothes:

Darlene and he had been married for nearly 12 years before Lindsey had come along. Due to some type of birth defect, Lindsey had been born without her left arm and only a partial right arm (which, eventually, had to be amputated because the bone in it was severely deformed and was causing their daughter agonizing pain). George had lost the total use of his right leg and only had partial use of his left leg after being involved in a car wreck.

Darlene is a stay-at-home mom who homeschools Lindsey (who should be in the 2nd grade but who is doing 4th grade work – that should sound familiar to any homeschooling parent) and George is on partial disability because he still teaches welding part-time and Lindsey loves to dance. They've been having a difficult time due to the fact that George can't teach full-time and they're still paying off medical bills related to Lindsey's rehab. Due to the cost of rehab, they'd lost the house they had lived in for nearly 10 years and they currently live in the trailer because of the kindness of Darlene's brother (whom I have since met and who is a terrific guy). To say that George was thankful I'd driven all the way from Mobile to deliver clothes to a little girl I'd never met would be an understatement.

After several minutes, Lindsey bounced back into the living room and she was absolutely beaming! Excitedly she asked if I wanted to see a 'new dance' she'd recently made up to one of her favorite songs. Of course I said "Yes."

Immediately she went to their stereo system, used her forehead to pop-open the glass doors and then took a pen in her mouth and began manipulating the controls on the stereo with amazing precision. Soon enough she'd found the track she wanted, pressed play and ran out into the middle of the living room. For several minutes Lindsey danced and pranced around the room, whirling and twirling so that the 'gypsy dress' flared out in different directions and made plumes of color around her caramel-colored legs. By the time Big Daddy Weave's Audience of One was done I was in tears but was smiling from ear to ear. I stayed at the trailer long enough for Lindsey to model each one of the dresses I'd brought for her.

After a few more hugs and being introduced to each one of their dogs I was escorted to my truck by the three of them, given one final snuggle by Lindsey and I was off to see someone in a local hospital.

As I drove away from their home I became completely overwhelmed by emotion and had to pull my truck over. I sat, alone in a parking lot, weeping. I wept not only because God had allowed me to make contact with such a precious family but also because my children are, by and large, whole.

I thought of the way Lindsey had danced with such joy and I realized that, after a few minutes of seeing her dancing, in my mind I was 'seeing' my own daughters hands and arms making motions in the air – fluid strokes of pure passion that I see her do almost every single day when she dances for my wife and I. Then I began crying more because I realized Lindsey doesn't recognize herself as 'handicapped' and, because of that, she really isn't.

I think it's rare for us to really know what we're thankful for. But, as for me, I know what I'm thankful for and it's more than the fact that God has given me healthy children. Rather, I'm thankful He has allowed me to become infected with His love for others and that He allows all of us who are willing to share His love with others and to meet people who will be eternally impacted by this love. We, in turn, are positively changed by the same.

My question to you is this: What are you thankful to God for?

℘

During the past twenty-five years Lonnie Honeycutt has served as the outreach minister for four churches. He has energetically sought to bring Jesus to those who are 'invisible' (the homeless, prostitutes, drug-users, those in nursing homes) and to those who have become disenfranchised by society. Ordained as a minister in 2006, Lonnie served briefly as the senior pastor of Deeper Life Fellowship East during which time he was diagnosed with Stage IV cancer of the head and neck and died on February 16, 2009 due to complications associated with his recovery. After being resurrected he wrote the well-received book *Death, Heaven and Back*. In 2010, he and his wife (Dawn) founded 99 for 1 Ministries – a non-profit organization dedicated to serving those who are under-loved. Currently Pastor Lonnie is working on his third book Living Jesus Out Loud for Families. He may be contacted for speaking engagements by visiting www.99for1Ministries.com or emailing him at: LivingJesusOutLoud@99for1Ministries.com.

Arthur's Poem

Submitted by David Brumbaugh

Arthur is a young man who was born in Russia with formidable birth defects of the arms and spine. He spent his formative years in an orphanage, and although the term "nightmarish" is typically used in hyperbole, it is truly an understatement of the conditions under which he was raised.

When he was eight years old he was adopted by an American couple with a younger daughter. The emotional trauma he had suffered in Russia was compounded by an abusive and adulterous adoptive father.

He went to live with a family in the Ozarks of Missouri where he became a dedicated Christian. As he told me, "Before I met Jesus, I knew right from wrong, I just didn't care".

His poetry shows the pain of one who as suffered physically and emotionally contrasted with the joy of one who knows he is truly loved by a Heavenly Father.

"MOURNING TO JOY"
by Arthur

All this pain has come
So Your will be done
Oh how I ache
And my heart does break

Why me, Lord?
Why the pain?
Mine sufferings
They do remain
A love that I, cannot feel
This grieving heart, I cannot steal

My body trembles, in my wake
Give me something, that I can take
To end this fear, to end this pain
My love is gone, and hate remains

Why me, Lord?
Why the pain?
Mine sufferings
They do remain

David Brumbaugh

A love that I, cannot feel
This grieving heart, I cannot steal

Why can't someone else be blamed?
So I can lash out, and soothe this pain
My thoughts are broken, my trust is gone
Courage shaken, my life is done

Why me, Lord?
Why the pain?
Mine sufferings
They do remain
A love that I, cannot feel
This grieving heart, I cannot steal

And my reality
Is not what it should be
I'll drown the sorrow
Must I wait for morrow?

Why me, Lord?
Why the pain?
Mine sufferings
They do remain
A love that I, cannot feel
This grieving heart, I cannot steal

Darkness threatens to surround me
Hatred in my heart's abounding

Just South of Forever

Terror grips my broken mind
I look for things I cannot find

Why me, Lord?
Why the pain?
Mine sufferings
They do remain
A love that I, cannot feel
This grieving heart, I cannot steal

And tears they stream, down my face
My swollen eyes, my head a daze
Life feels crumbled, around me
Incapable of love, am I to be?

Why me, Lord?
Why the pain?
Mine sufferings
They do remain
A love that I, cannot feel
This grieving heart, I cannot steal

Is this a test?
Is this a joke?
A broken mess
Please give me hope

Why me, Lord?
Why the pain?

David Brumbaugh

Mine sufferings
They do remain
A love that I, cannot feel
This grieving heart, I cannot steal

I had a recollection
That reached my inner heart
That God gave me redemption
My heart pierced like a dart

Your everlasting love
Like a gracious dove
Tamed the angry beast in me
It is joy that I now see

Oh my God
A Shepherd with a rod
And we the sheep for you
To be gallantly pursued

Your everlasting love
Like a gracious dove
Tamed the angry beast in me
It is joy that I now see

Holy glorious Father
I've walked in my pain
But now I would rather
Follow You again

Just South of Forever

Your everlasting love
Like a gracious dove
Tamed the angry beast in me
It is joy that I now see

You are more than anything
Beyond compare
You're indescribable
And uncontainable

Your everlasting love
Like a gracious dove
Tamed the angry beast in me
It is joy that I now see

Glorious father, brilliant light
Giver of freedom, provider of life
You are the only one I need
Because of You I am set free

Your everlasting love
Like a gracious dove
Tamed the angry beast in me
It is joy that I now see

OLDSMOBILE

by Gary Morris

"It's not your father's Oldsmobile."

Do you remember that television commercial from the late 1980's? My dad drove Oldsmobiles beginning in the late fifties. Specifically, he drove Ninety-Eight models. Ninety-Eight was the name of that particular model of Oldsmobile. I can remember at least 5 that he owned.

We had a ditch on one side of our back yard, and he would lay out a couple of thick planks across it, drive his Olds 98 up on there, and change the oil.

He did it that way for a couple of good reasons. One, it was a heck of a lot easier and more comfortable than when he used to crawl up under it on the patio. On the patio, there was very little clearance to get under the car. In the ditch, he could almost stand up while draining the oil pan and changing the filter, and he would also grease the Alemite fittings.

He probably performed more services than that, except I didn't stay around to watch. I was usually busy playing with the beagles, waging war with my Daisy Red Ryder, or shootin' hoops. Which brought about the other reason he quit changing the oil on the patio.

One hot June day, while I was merrily having a hoopfest on my own, dad decided it was time to change the oil in his car. I used to love looking under the hood at that monster 455 Oldsmobile Rocket engine. Talk about a land ship! Riding in those cars was like riding on a cloud with a team of wild horses harnessed to it. Pure metal, with a gagged banshee between the front wheels!

Dad set up his equipment and began to crawl underneath. "Don't bounce that ball around here, now," he said as he slid the plastic basin used for the oil reservoir underneath the car. He'd drain the old oil out into it, then pour into another container to be taken to a gas station where they'd dispose of it for him. He'd repeat himself every time he thought he heard that basketball getting close. Each time his tone was a little firmer, and a little higher, "Don't bounce that ball around here now!"

I was Pistol Pete, Wilt the Stilt and Lew Alcindor all rolled into one short, fat white boy, busting goals and burning nets. Actually, I was a great shot. I could even do the mighty "sky hook" (and still can today!) That day, man, I was on! I was hitting everything, from everywhere. I was even standing behind my goal and making shots over the top from behind, and underneath the awning at the corner of the house–granny-style–from 20 feet!

Dad finally finished changing the oil, and slid the used oil reservoir out from under his 1972 Ninety-Eight Regency. His feet and most of his legs were sticking out from under the front end, as he tightened the oil pan bolt and rechecked the filter.

Meanwhile back on the concrete court, like a rude awakening to a sweet dream, an errant shot glanced off the rim and high-bounced in the direction of that oil basin. I can still see the slow motion, instant replay in my mind. I can taste the sweat even now. There was only one thing to do–run that ball down–that wicked Spalding, which was hell-bent on going right into that oil!

I sprinted as fast as any kid ever did. One bounce, two bounces. The fourth landing of the third bounce was going to be drowned in 10W-40! I lunged for the ball. Smack! I caught it midair between third bounce and splashdown.

YES! I did it! I saved the ball! Woo hoo for me! But, what was the uniquely odd feeling I had, engulfing my right foot? The instant replay is still spinning. In my mind's eye, I can still see that oil reservoir flying up from one corner, having been catapulted into the air by my size 6 Converse, oil going all over it and my white crew socks, all over the side of that beautiful Oldsmobile, the concrete around, and . . . oh no . . . dad's legs!

I quickly dodged off the side of the patio, leaving oily, right-side-only footprints. My shoe and socks now needed an oil change.

I heard Daddy mutter a few words, some unintelligible, some profane, as he hit his head 3 or 4 times trying to get out from under the car. "Dang it boy, I told you not to play with that basketball around here!", he said as his head finally cleared the undercarriage. Both of his pant-leg bottoms were soaked with Quaker State, socks too. Thankfully, he had on his old "brogan" boots as he called them, which were already so soiled that the oil just ran off them like water off a duck's back.

"I'm sorry dad!" "I'm sorry," I said as he looked at his feet and the oil everywhere.

I had already turned to go put the basketball up. My showcase was over. I knew he was mad. No, I knew he was furious. I didn't realize how upset he had gotten. In one of the only two times I ever got any physical punishment from daddy, this was the second time, and I never saw it coming.

As I walked across the patio (with only my left shoe on at this time, mind you) I suddenly felt myself being launched from the ground. I actually came back into orbit and touched down before even I realized the pain of having been kicked squarely in the hind parts with a size 10-1/2 "brogan."

Well, we had a mess on our hands. And on our feet! But the biggest mess I reckon was, in dad's mind, the mess he made of us. He came and found me in my room a few hours later, sulking, sitting sideways on my bed (I sure couldn't sit fully on my backside!)

I guess it weighed pretty heavily on dad, because not only did he apologize profusely, he kept the promise he made that day perfectly--he never, ever laid another finger on me. There were plenty of times when he should have. And he certainly could have, especially in the days before his hip replacements and melanoma.

But dad became more peaceful. And more peaceable. I don't know what happened that day, but he sure changed. I guess he was able to see something about himself that he didn't like. He was sort of a visionary that way. I say that's why he traded his last Oldsmobile for a Buick, just a couple of years before the Oldsmobile brand was discontinued from General Motors' lineup. I couldn't believe it–he'd

ALWAYS owned Oldsmobile Ninety-Eights, for at least 40 years.

But daddy always knew when it was time for a change. Just like the oil in those Oldsmobiles. And relocating his working area from the patio to the ditch. And a change of his heart and attitude.

Thanks, dad, for the great example.

☙

Gary Morris is an American writer, currently residing in Mobile, Alabama. He is an accomplished writer, editor and publisher, having contributed articles and published magazines in the choral music field and the residential real estate industry. Although trained in all facets of publishing, he prefers to invest his time in writing humorous, heartfelt, and down home fiction and nonfiction pieces. He is currently working on a collection of stories for a men's devotional project.

The Possum in the Road

by Stephen Simpson

WARNING: Do not read while eating. Especially if eating marsupials. Also, do not read if you are offended by my incorrect spelling of "opossum".

In our family, relaxation is very hard work. It is a known fact that no matter when we try to go on a vacation, and no matter where, there will be a major construction project beginning at our hotel corresponding with our arrival. Or possibly a hurricane. Back when my wife, Susanne, and I were celebrating our Twenty-Fifth Wedding Anniversary, the country we wanted to visit was suddenly shrouded in clouds of volcanic ash from a massive eruption.

I think that major resorts, and possibly nations, should

pay us to stay away.

Before our anniversary trip, however, on the actual date of our Silver Wedding Anniversary, Susanne and I planned a quiet day together, with a lovely lunch scheduled overlooking Mobile Bay. As I was preparing to meet her, I received a phone call from my college-aged daughter, Gracie, who was driving home from class. Her tearful voice on the other end of the line startled me.

"Daddy, where are you?"

"I'm at home, what's wrong?" No parent wants to hear their daughter crying on the phone when she is supposed to be arriving home. I braced for bad news.

"Oh, Daddy, it's terrible!"

"Honey, where are you? What's wrong?"

"Daddy, somebody here in the neighborhood had an accident and ...."

Dramatic pause.

"Daddy, somebody has hit a possum with their car."

Long exhale from Dad. She continued:

"But, it's a Momma possum, and she's dead, and there are possum babies coming out and they are running into the street, and I am trying to keep cars from hitting them."

Now, some people may have heard my sermon about "The Turtle in the Road," where God spoke to me through the dilemma of a poor, helpless terrapin. (Note: God did not speak to me through the turtle; only through the situation. Let us be clear.) At any rate, the acorn has not fallen far from the tree, as my daughter apparently shares our family predilection for rescuing animals in danger. Understand, it isn't every day you get to celebrate your 25th Anniversary, and I didn't want to delay or miss my hot date. Especially not for a possum. I don't like possums, except maybe with rice and brown gravy.

Of course, it wasn't about the possum. My girl needed her Daddy, so within minutes, I was standing next to her in the road, directing traffic and corralling four wayward baby possums. I was also working the cell phone, calling "Animal Control" for assistance. As it turns out, "Animal Control" said that they didn't handle "wild animals," which was a major newsflash to me.

Thank God for an understanding wife, who was already waiting for me at the restaurant, but agreed to postpone our wonderful date until I could resolve this crisis. After all, she's not just a great wife, but a loving Mom who felt the concerns of our daughter.

Soon, my own Dad was in on the rescue as well, bringing me a much-needed box and some high-tech possum extraction equipment (paper towels). I put all of this to use in gathering up the four little possum babies who were just starting to open their eyes, and they were making tiny heart-rending yelps. My heart could be moved by possums. Who knew?

I soon discovered that there were four more baby possums that were "not yet delivered". Oh my! For the sake of the squeamish, I will fast-forward the story and say that I tenderly placed eight healthy newborn possums into the box and prepared for a rushed drive to an environmental study center which specializes in care for wounded or imperiled animals.

As I prepared to leave, I thanked my father and hugged my daughter. She grabbed me tight and through a teary smile said, "Well, Daddy, now you can do a sermon about "The Possum in the Road."

Love is an amazing motivator, especially the love of a parent for their child. Love is not only expressed in the spectacular – such as possum rescues – but in being available and engaged in living life together from day-to-day. It is in being willing to sacrifice what is precious or enjoyable for you to be in situations that may be unpleasant or difficult – for the sake of blessing or helping the people you love.

Jesus taught us to pray to God, "our Father." In Luke 11, Jesus said that if earthly fathers desire to do good for their children, how much more will our Heavenly Father give us good gifts, including the precious gift of the Holy Spirit? He said in Matthew 6 that if the Heavenly Father takes care of the birds, how much more will He care for His children?

Those who have received Jesus Christ by faith now have the nature of the Father living within them. John tells us that "God is love." Father God not only expresses His love to us, but also through us. And love is the greatest lesson that we can teach our children.

Love is costly. Love can be messy. Love makes you reach. Love is not convenient. Love is often not expressed on your own terms. Love will cause you to care for possum babies on your Silver Wedding Anniversary.

Speaking of the Anniversary, within an hour of my documentary-worthy possum adventure, I was cleaned up and seated across the table from my lovely wife enjoying her company, the cuisine, and the bayside view. We survived that anniversary and, thank the Lord, nothing happened to the restaurant while we were there.

Our 30th Anniversary is coming up in a couple of years, and we've been thinking of visiting Maine. Somebody needs to warn New England that we are coming!

CR

Stephen Simpson is a writer and editor based in southern Alabama. He has served in pastoral ministry for more than 30 years and is the editor of *One-to-One Magazine*, an award-winning international quarterly produced by CSM Publishing. Stephen received his Bachelor of Arts in Communications - Journalism from Spring Hill College in 1984, and also studied at Reformed Theological Seminary and Liberty Ministry Training Institute. He is the Managing Editor of *The Covenant & the Kingdom* Bible Study Curriculum and serves on the Executive Council of Opportunity for Unity. Stephen has been featured on numerous radio and television programs, and he speaks at churches, conferences, and camps, as well as at Covenant Church of Mobile, where he is Senior Pastor. He resides in the Mobile area, with his wife, Susanne. They have one adult daughter.

SOPHIA

by Candy Reid

"The power of life and death are in the tongue, And they that love it will eat its fruit."

-Proverbs 18:21

In Isaiah 45:3 God declares, "I will give you the treasures of darkness and hidden riches of secret places, that you may know that I, the Lord, who call you by your name, Am the God of Israel." I've journeyed through many dark places in my life: breast cancer and the resulting treatment and surgery, a debilitating neurological disorder in one of my children, betrayal at the hands of a trusted friend, financial difficulties...you get the picture. One thing I learned early in my relationship with the Lord is that He is always faithful. Every situation in which I found myself, no matter how dark and daunting, would always be a place that harbored treasure upon treasure just waiting to be discovered. Nuggets of wisdom that would draw me closer to Him; beckoning me to rest in His perfect peace; gifting me with His truths to share with others.

I have always been amazed and blessed beyond measure as God entrusted me with valuable spiritual treasures in circumstances over which I had no control. But I have been overwhelmed with gratitude that God, in his infinite mercy and kindness, would choose to extract for me treasures from the shadowy places of my own shameful self-righteousness.

One such gem was given many years ago not long after I'd become a Christian. I worked in the administrative department of a high-end retail company. My office manager's name was Sophia. From all outward appearances we didn't seem to be likely candidates for a friendship. Sophia was in her 50's while I was only a couple of years past my 20th birthday. She had been married for over thirty years. Myself, only four. She had raised three children and even had a couple of grandchildren, whereas I was just beginning my journey into parenthood with one toddler. She smoked cigarettes constantly; one after another. I had quit four years before I met her and couldn't even stand the smell of the "nasty things". Sophia loved the fulfillment found in running the office efficiently. I simply punched the time clock to earn a pay check while my heart yearned to be at home with my son.

In spite of our differences we formed a fast friendship that extended beyond the walls of our dank, windowless office. We found lots to laugh about and didn't hesitate to share our hearts with one another. We stayed in touch even after my dream of being a stay-at-home mom became a reality.

One day a couple of years after I made my exit from the professional world my phone rang. It was Sophia. I knew by the sound of her voice that something was wrong. She shared with me that tests from a recent doctor's visit had revealed a spot on her lung and that the doctor was "concerned". I can't recall the remainder of our conversation, but I remember how I felt after I hung up the phone. I was scared. And angry. I was scared that Sophia could soon be taken from me and I wasn't ready. I was angry that she had intentionally made choices over the years that had harmed her body and now she was facing the consequences – consequences that would ultimately affect those who loved her. Why hadn't she thought ahead? Didn't she know that smoking would kill her? Hadn't I tried to get her to stop over and over?

In my sorrow and frustration I cried out to God, begging Him for her healing, asking that her addiction finally be broken. I also thanked Him that I wasn't so bound by an addiction that I would be unwilling to abandon it even when I knew it was causing damage to my body. As I was praying I felt the words, 'The power of life and death are in the tongue' resonate through my spirit. I thought it odd that such a strange sounding phrase would meander through my mind while I was having a serious conversation with God. On and off throughout the day that phrase continued to make its way into my thoughts. In keeping with the pharisaical attitude that had prompted my "Thank you" prayer, it did not even occur to me that God was trying to tell me something. Finally, when those same words came to me the next day during my prayer time I began to reason that maybe this wasn't just a coincidence. I was still a fairly new Christian and as far as I could remember there was nothing in the Bible that talked about power in the tongue, but I decided to break out the concordance just in case. And, lo and behold, there it was! Right there in Proverbs. Not only did Solomon say that the power of life and death are in the tongue, he goes on to basically say that you eat what you speak.

As the truth of this scripture poured through my spirit I was slammed with the recognition of my own self-righteousness. I was suddenly aware of the many times I had shared a prayer request with a sister in Christ without allowing myself to acknowledge that it was nothing more than thinly-veiled gossip. Wasn't I guilty of discussing how dreadful some people's housekeeping skills were? Allowing myself to be fooled into thinking it was acceptable because I ended the discussion with "Bless her heart". How often did I participate in a conversation where someone's personal information was shared without their knowledge or consent? Maybe I wasn't smoking a pack or two of cigarettes each day, but I was definitely sowing death by the words that proceeded out of my own mouth.

As I allowed the light of the scripture to expose the ugliness of my sin I had to acknowledge that I had an addiction just as Sophia and so many others did. Only my addiction harmed the spirit and the soul. With shame I recognized that I enjoyed knowing the 'inside scoop'. I was faced with the repulsive realization that there was a twisted boost to my self-esteem when I discussed the shortcomings of others. Compared to the homes of some women I knew, my not-so-clean house looked like an entry for a Better Homes and Gardens contest. Having a confidential conversation about that privileged information with a few other ladies only served to build me up.

G.u.i.l.t.y. I was guilty. And, oh, I was so ashamed. With tears of repentance I confessed to God what He already knew and immediately I was wrapped in His forgiving embrace.

I still slip sometimes. And I'm often tempted to say more than I should, but I am quick to listen to the Holy Spirit's prompting in this area. I'll even risk looking foolish by stopping mid-sentence and saying, "Sorry, but I really shouldn't be talking about this." And, I must admit, I've even had to revisit a conversation with a confession that I was wrong.

This unexpected treasure of truth has taught me to carefully measure the words that I speak; always being aware that what I speak WILL produce fruit. Whether that fruit is life or death is determined by my own tongue. What kind of fruit will you see produced from the words of your mouth? It's a heavy question, I know. But it's a question that begs to be examined. I encourage you to be willing to allow God to show you areas in which the words of your mouth aren't sowing life.

Candy Reid, mom to 4 and wife to the love of her life, is a gifted encourager who seeks to seize every opportunity to inspire others in their walk with God. A firm believer that the simple things in life are the most precious, Candy adores the sound of her children's laughter, coffee and conversation with a true-blue friend, and holding hands with her hubby on the backyard swing. And chocolate. Definitely chocolate. You can contact her via email at: embracingthetrials@yahoo.com.

The Life of a Flower

by Jessica Laurie

You, little seed, are going to grow.

Though all you see is the dirt of the earth around you, the Gardener will nurture you and help you grow into what he planted you to be. Even though you can't see Him from where you are, He's taking care of you.

You see, He planted you in just the right spot to receive all the sunlight you need. He's watering you so that you receive nourishment. He's watching to see if you will respond and come up out of the earth to greet Him. He so wants to see you.

Ah, there you are!

Sprouting from the earth was a brave and daring thing to do, but necessary. If you had not, you would not have lived.

Now, behold the Gardener! He's smiling down at you, glad that you chose to grow to see Him.

You look around tentatively, noticing other flowers and shoots that are surrounding you.

They seem bigger somehow, more ready to face the elements of the world and more worthy to grace the Gardener's beautiful garden.

Fear not.

The Gardener waters you and works the ground around you tenderly.

All of the other seeds experienced the same growing period you are going through. Each is going through a different stage of growth at this moment.

As you become more comfortable in this new world, this garden, you grow even more.

You see the sunlight and feel its warmth. You taste the drops of water, feel the air, and thrive under the

Gardener's care.
You stretch upward.

Hard rain beats you down.

You shudder, shrinking back, not knowing how harsh water could be. You look for the

Gardener. Where is He? Why doesn't He stop this rain that wants to batter you into the ground?

He's here. Don't worry. He knows how much you can handle.

The Gardener sees the whole process. He's with you through it all.

He's protecting you on those cold, fierce nights when you think you can't survive. He is covering you and keeping you warm, making sure the frost won't touch you.

On hot, dry days when you don't have the strength to lift your head and you think you

could just wilt away, He's watering you and refreshing your strength.

When it seems no one notices you, the Gardener

is singing over you, filling you with His breath, causing you to stretch higher to meet His voice.

And you grow.

Oh, His delight when you bloom, little flower! His joy and pleasure made the growing process worthwhile.

But, oh, how brief is the bloom of a flower. How very short is its life. A single flash of color in a kaleidoscope of rainbows. A brief moment in the span of time.

But to the Gardener, a perfect time. A perfect moment.

As you start to wilt, dear flower, as you know the time when your stems, leaves, and petals are about return to the dust, you remember your life.

As you look back, you see that though the bloom of your life was a joyful, lovely time, your favorite part was when you were growing, though at the time it didn't seem so. For when you were growing was when you grew to know the Gardener best. The growing is what made the bloom possible.

As you wilt, sweet flower, know your life was not in vain, no matter how brief or trivial it may have seemed.

The Gardener planted you, took care of you, helped you grow.

And in growing into what you were planted to be, you brought Him joy.

Now, as you return to the dust, you see even more.

The Gardener has cultivated the ground around you. The seeds that you have borne in your life as you grew are now taking on their own life as they meet the earth and rise out of it under the Gardener's caring hand.

Oh, rejoice, little flower!

You have been and are forever part of the fragrance of heaven, and you are the delight and dearly loved of the Gardener.

Jessica Laurie is a homeschool graduate and a graduate from the University of South Alabama with a major in English and a minor in Music. She has had various pieces published, including a short story in a Fine Arts magazine, and a children's book, The Voyage of the Merry Jane that was adapted into an original ballet. She is also a part of Team Novel Teen, a group of writers, readers, and bloggers who promote clean, teen fiction. Jessica's debut young adult novel will be released in 2013 from Wyatt House Publishing.

WEAVING A TAPESTRY OF LOVE
AND OTHER POEMS

by Katie Stuckas

Don't think it possible for one to lack this priceless jewel

Nor believe a heart should break because it cannot heal

There is a place within each one, a depth, but from above

That holds the thread from God's own hand

To weave a tapestry of love He uses all the things we think are bland, or not with sense

To sew these threads together that will form our life's blueprint

The window to a heart, or passers by who've yet to see

He claims it all, and sets us up for all eternity

A letter written years before, or aged pics of old

Even mama's praying hands, or a battle on a boat

Neither wood, nor hay nor stubble can be used for His desire

It's only what is in the heart, the 'depth' that's seen the fire

A gentle rebuke; yes, this is love; He'll use to mold His plan

The shelter of His love is endless, for He's the great "I AM"

So take this priceless gift to heart, for God's at work above

To liken us into His way, as He weaves this tapestry of love

༄

THE WINDOW TO YOUR HEART

While flying through the field one day, in search of food to eat

A bird took note of something that before, she'd not yet seen

A house was standing by itself; beside it, a running brook

The bird, though cautious at the first, flew in for a closer look

Surveying her most recent find, the bird began to chance

A little closer to the house, now grounded she did prance

The hunger pains she felt within were more than she could bear

For in her former nesting home, no food could be found there

The land was parched and fading fast; new growth was not in sight

So, desperate for a morsel bit, she flew with all her might

Drawing nearer to the house, an oddity she found

A window, usually built up high, sat kissing at the ground

Her curiosity unleashed, she no more could still

And with a giant hop or two, gave her rest upon the sill

By this time her heart beat fast with fear, but too, with hope

If only she would find a bite to strengthen her weary soul

Alas! But could this ever be; no, surely but a dream

She gazed a little closer; yes! Her eyes beheld the seed

Another rarity she thought, 'my work is well with ease'

For looking at the window, she found an open seam

With a bit of nervousness, she felt the need to risk

And squeeze a bit between the molds to fulfill her biggest wish

At last she grasped the food in hand; t'was sweet, for more she yearned

But fearing hurt or danger thought, tomorrow I'll return

Just South of Forever

Thus began the pleasant flight each day to take her feast

And every time she perched the sill, she entered more with ease

The seeds of life to feed her soul, did ever more grow larger

Until at last she felt at peace; she knew she found safe harbor

One day while flying through a field to gather her daily food

The bird took note of something odd, that once for her, was good

Below her wings she saw a land, once parched and fading fast

Was suddenly about with life, and pleasing to look at

The bird then thought within herself of all those days ago

When going to that window sill, to feed her weary soul

She would eat her fill of food, and when she was satisfied

Would take the rest and find a place where she, the food would hide

Now every day when she looks back to what that seed has built

She's thankful for the owner who claims the window and the sill

❧

Katie Stuckas

THE BUS STOP

He was standing at the bus stop, when she came walking by

The way he tipped his hat to her somehow caught her eye

She wondered who he could have been; he wondered of her, the same

Then just before the bus pulled up, he turned and asked her name

"They call me Liza," she replied, and reached to shake his hand

Her touch went deep into his heart; he said, "My name is Sam"

The conversation took them back, to forty years ago

When both were living out their dreams of love, success and hope

She told him of her pageant days and when she won the crown

He shared his nights of playing ball, and scoring the big touchdown

She talked about the big gray house that stood on fourth and vine

And how she carved her name into the tree when she was nine

Without a pause, he said to her, "I know about that place"

"I lived there many years ago, but moved when I was eight"

Suddenly his mind went back; he thought of that old tree

He smiled at her and swallowed hard, then said "How can this be?"

She looked at him and for a time her memory rang true

She chose her word with care, then said "I can't believe it's you"

The memories came flooding back, when on that rainy day

They stood beside the tree and cried, while carving both their names

The breakup took him far from home, but she and mom stayed there

That tree seemed like the only bond the two of them would share

Three buses now had passed them by; they'd lost all track of time

And then without a hesitance, they walked to fourth and vine

The tree was like an eery ghost; it stood there in the night

And though the rain was falling hard, to them it all felt right

The two stood there together, Sam holding Liza's hand

Then he took out his knife and carved these words: 'Together Again'

Katie Stuckas

Iris's Love Letter

She took off her coat, hung it there by the door

Stepped softly across the old hardwood floor

Then just like the day when she first saw his face

She stared at the note lying there by the vase

The letter was wrapped in a ribbon of blue

She smiled as she counted the small 'I love you's'

Then walking toward that old rocking chair

She opened the letter to read what was there

"My love for you is deeper than the red of a rose

My love for you is longer than any of God's rainbows

Iris my love, for you I will wait, as long as forever, as long as it takes

Meet me tomorrow at our secret place; I'm counting the minutes

'Til we can embrace

She opened her eyes to the clock by her bed

She looked at the numbers; a deep crimson red

Just South of Forever

Then just like the day when he gave her his name

She started to cry; then remembered the dream

She slipped on her shoes, felt her way to the trunk

Looked deep inside, amid all the junk

There at the bottom, in a ribbon of blue

Was the letter he wrote her from 1932

She ran outside, the note clutched to her chest

Made her way up the hill to the place of his rest

She thought back in time when he first met her there

It was their secret place for so many years

The grass was still wet from the rain hours ago

She noticed the sky; a beautiful rainbow

Then just like the day when she told him goodbye

She opened the letter, and read while she cried

ℰ

Katie Stuckas

PICTURE THIS

I took out that old picture frame of mom and dad today

The color, although black and white, had barely begun to fade

I tried to picture in my mind of how and when they met

The year was fifty seven when they decided to wed

The picture bore some wrinkles from years of wear and tear

But even time could not erase the love that was seen there

The struggles of their youth 'til now you see, were not in vain

For God has blessed four children to hold the family name

Today that picture perfect love is fifty six years old

Mom and dad share memories no picture frame can hold

And time has carefully portrayed their life of love and bliss

And I'm amazed, but thankful, that I can picture this

MAMA'S PRAYING HANDS

I would hear her voice in the darkness, amid the fall of
the rain

Not understanding all she said, but knowing just the
same

A small child, young and innocent, outside her door I'd
stand

And wait with eager patience, to see mama's praying
hands

Standing by the side of her bed, she'd look to God on high

Then slowly she would bend her knees, cup her hands
and cry

Her words would send me flying like the winds upon the
sand

The tears flowed like sweet honey, over mama's praying
hands

Today, no longer that small child, having ways that are
my own

The memories still stain my heart of those nights so long
ago

For now, I pray like mama, and I've come to understand

That what I saw was childlike faith, in mama's praying
hands

Battle On the Boat to Zanzibar

(Salvation's quest)

The desert ocean traveled clear blue, consumed with hurriedness

Only small pockets of calm prevailed, as many toured obligations

They floated cautiously, the dead and the living, mixed among shifting waters

How sure are the feet of the living!

She sat quiet in her seat, a heart of stone, native among foreign creatures of light

Darkness fumbled for position, hovering before eyes of mercy;

A spiritual battle ensued.

How calm her appearance played to the shrieking of her soul; a prideful course

Deception shadowed her mind, hidden only by traditional garb.

Sweet freedom lurked, the sacrifice placed before her now.

A sense of death awakened, then buckled helplessly as victory took its place

Flesh cowered, falling, jumping into light

Blood soaked her being, like marrow swallows bones; drenching blood,

innocent blood, pure of heart.

Oh, the depth of that soaking!

Faith lifted her head, as grace found her without doom

The battle over, life had conquered death

Taste and see! Only to die is to live

❧

LOVE NEVER FAILS

Her speech was firm but gentle,

Each rebuke like snow falling on winter's bloom

Wisdom hung about her neck; a priceless stone

Calm stayed the room as they talked,

No clanging symbols emerged from the corner

The older taught the younger;

Each heart a different spiritual rung

Hidden treasure was waiting to be found-

The search, a masterpiece of intrigue

Patience whispered through words of absolute truth;

Truth that determined a destiny

This woman of Godly years held love unfailing in her hands-

A love that mirrored scars of long ago

THIS IS LOVE

"What is love," I heard him say, while sitting in the park today

I took his hand and whispered low, "I'll tell you everything you need to know

Love is patient, true and kind, love says this is 'ours' not 'mine'

Love keeps a promise that is made, love doesn't lie, is never swayed"

"Why do you ask," I finally said; he looked at me and shook his head

"I lived those words for sixty years," the old man smiled and wiped his tears

"My wife was everything you say; forgive my tears, but she died today

I did the very best I could, to give her love the way I should

Today, your words help me to rest, in knowing that I did my best

And now, I have no doubt she knew; for sixty years, what love was too"

IN THE SHELTER OF HIS LOVE

Let me tell you of a place, that's built on solid ground

A refuge I can call my own, where peace and joy abound

I dwell within the Most High, Who watches from above

I hide beneath His feathers, in the shelter of His love

My protector and provider, how he guards my every step

Sending angels to uplift me, in His hands I need not fret

I can rest within His shadow, for He Who watches o'er the dove

Keeps me ever more from harm, in the shelter of His love

❧

"I AM"

"I AM" has waited for you; Everlasting love came quick for your heart

"I AM" everlasting! I will chase you far, long, no matter the depth or height

You are forever engraved, etched in my hand, for "I AM" formed you; a longing

Never ending! Choose this lover, and no other; I wait patiently, for "I AM"

❧

There are different flows to love, different expressions, different rhythms to love that can be seen, felt, heard and spoken. In the end, love is all that remains, no matter how it is conveyed. "But now faith, hope, love, abide these three; but the greatest of these is love."

You see, love always wins. Love is why we are here.

CR

Katie Stuckas started her writing journey in 1988, when she saw a heartbreaking television commercial about children starving. Her heart was moved in such a way that even today, her emotions from personal experiences, prayer, her relationship with God and others, has fueled the writing muse within. Katie has had numerous poems published through the Poetry Guild, and was even nominated as Poet Ambassador two different years. Her poetry has awarded her the coveted 'Editor's Choice' award four times through The International Library of Poetry. Katie also writes short skits and dramas, two of which were performed at churches in the Mobile area. Along with her poetry gift, Katie has also written and put together a cookbook, which was used to raise money for Africa Missions. A local TV station found out about her project, and requested an interview, calling it a "labor of love." Katie was also asked in 2010 to provide her writing expertise on a movie script that was being written by a playwright from California. Katie also does editing work, and just recently was consulted and asked to help edit a future training manual on transformation, due out in late 2013.

Better Than Jesus

by Jennifer Lopes

(Excerpted from *"God of the Gray Areas"*)

I was trying to be better than Jesus. Of course I didn't know it at the time, but it would be revealed to me later. You see, I was going through a very difficult time when my neighbor was constantly harassing my children. They were being confronted and reprimanded for playing ball and as the hill would serve them, the ball often rolled into their yard. We built a batting cage to enjoy and hoped it might also limit the number of times the ball would go next door. Then we found ourselves under the threat of a law suit for the batting cage, despite it being in our own backyard. Things escalated when we had the cops called to us for - yes, you are going to read it correctly - for shooting basketball in the cul-de-sac in the middle of a summer day! This happened several times and culminated when the neighbor referred to my son as a "Christian" mockingly. Then she resorted to calling him a "Mother of a Something". Except she used the real words. This fifty-something buffoon, yet seemingly sophisticated-type, topped it off by doing a dancing gorilla imitation toward him (he was only 12).

We ended up pressing charges. When the case made its way to court, the inexperienced city attorney never called our other witnesses and closed her arguments before ever asking my son if she said those things to him. Our verbal abusing neighbor, on the other hand, had a hired attorney that reminded us of a grizzly Mr. Noodle. He relished in his witnesses' lies and spin. Needless to say - she was found "not guilty." Did this Judge's ruling change the truth of what really happened? No. Did I feel for a moment that God had surely allowed justice to fall in the street? Of course. And I was willing to take matters into my own hands. And so I did.

I came home from court ready to avenge my children. I started documenting all behavior. Building my case became my focus. I even had a law firm eager to take the case, pro bono, to seek recompense for my family. Until one day, a friend of mine stopped by to pray with me. She started her prayer with the intention (I had hoped) to pray against my neighbor and that God would move them out of our neighborhood. Honestly, I would've been fine if He would have chosen to move them to another state or country. After all, we were ministers of the Lord and this type of behavior shouldn't be allowed to happen to us, right?

Well, my friend began to pray and before I knew it... she was petitioning God for all sorts of blessings of mercy and grace. She prayed that love from strangers would be poured out on my neighbor. She began to weep and I, well, I, became angry. She prayed harder. Meanwhile, my anger grew. "Lord, promote them on their jobs," she cried. "Give them financial stability..." It went on and on. I, on the other hand, felt betrayed and told God I would not participate in the prayer. My friend then said the words that will forever convict me. "Lord, it is because of your goodness that men are drawn to repentance," she sobbed. I instantly had a vision of the Judge's mouth as she had formed the words, "Not guilty." It became clear to me. That day He manifested His goodness in that verdict - undeserved mercy. I began to weep over God's goodness. He allowed the inexperienced attorney to make a flop of herself. He allowed Mr. Noodle to parade his best game. God, the only true Judge, was, after all...in hot pursuit of my neighbor. His goodness was inescapable.

God was being "good" to her by allowing her to get off scot-free and suffer no consequences legally. He was drawing them to repentance. He knew that He could trust us with the pain of being made out to be fabricators. She on the other hand, needed God to be revealed to her in a major way. I began to weep further over the spiritual condition of a grown woman that would verbally attack young children. I began to see her soul the way God sees her soul. Her soul was at the very least, sick, and at the most....lost and headed for an eternity of separation from Him, unless she turns her life over to Him.

I determined that day to cancel the free lawyers, throw out my scorekeeping notepad and turn it over to The Judge completely. It was clear to me that I had been "kicking against the goads" by opposing her and her foul attitude. I was trying to be better than Jesus. You see, the Bible is clear. Jesus said, "If the world hates you, you know that it hated me before it hated you. If you were of the world, the world would love its own....A servant is not greater than his master. If they persecuted me, they will also persecute you....they hated me without a cause." I began to embrace the thought of being attacked for prayer. I began to embrace the notion that someone would mock my Christianity. I began to realize that I was striving, as a servant, to be better than my master - Jesus. I repented. I stopped fighting the opposition. I now say, "Bring it on." I want to be in the company of Jesus - persecution and all. And I certainly don't want to pretend that I am better than Him.

I had a friend who once got blessed with a sharp, new luxury vehicle. She would arrive at work early to park her car in the back parking lot. She would literally pounce onto the pavement and zip across the asphalt to the door. You would have thought there were mud puddles and hail storms from the way she bolted to and from her car. I found out that she did this in an effort not to be seen by her other co-workers. When I asked her why she was behaving so secretly, she said that she didn't want to be questioned about her new car and was concerned that it might make other people jealous. She wholeheartedly thought it would make others feel badly that they didn't have a new car. Her line of thinking troubled me. She thought she was being lowly. In reality she actually had herself on her mind in excess.

There is a thing called false humility. It is when you or I attempt to be humble to the point of transgression. When you or I habitually "stay out of the fight" it reflects a fundamental perversion of what the Bible teaches. We are called to take sides and to take a stance against unrighteousness. Isaiah 1:17 (New International Version)... learn to do right! Seek justice, encourage the oppressed. Defend the cause of the fatherless, plead the case of the widow. (Rebuke the oppressor).

I now recognize that a lot of Christians fail to do this. I, personally, have determined not to shirk my responsibilities any longer. When we neglect to do what the scriptures tell us because it might hurt someone's feelings or look like we are being critical - it is basically pride- reversed and turned inwardly. It does not represent authentic humility.

I think we may have neglected this aspect of the Christian frontier.

For instance, if someone crosses a boundary in our lives that is clearly against what our Bible teaches us- why do we park in the back parking lot regarding the subject? Why do we avoid the confrontation? I think it is possible that we are afraid that we will be accused of "showing off" our faith (new car) or passing judgment (where is your new car?). Meanwhile, we are the one trapped in the cycle of "self." My friend was consumed with herself and it led to all kinds of illogical behavior. She tried so hard not to draw attention to herself. The opposite actually happened and her problems only grew. She would never muster the courage to confront her perception of how people saw her. Believe me- when you allow the devil to make you feel guilty for God's blessings... you have problems. It is oppression.

The Bible says that we should speak up for those that cannot speak for themselves, yet, some of us, like my friend, walk in a degree of false holiness causing us to excuse ourselves and turn our heads in every situation. We not only disenfranchise our internal, God-given anger about injustice, moreover, we suppress Godly protest. This is where you and I inadvertently are trying to "be better than Jesus." May I go further? I would dare to say that when we are obliging in our actions when a true injustice has occurred, that God is actually dishonored. I would dare to call it outright, sin. It is outside of the scope of His Word. I know this is a difficult concept. You may have to read it a couple of times for it to penetrate.

Let me tell you what might have prevented the entire escapade with my neighbor. If I would've seen that my children were being harassed undeservingly, I should have been standing on the property line the first time it happened and should have demanded that it never happen again- on the authority of God's Word. I think that is what Jesus would've done. I think that He would have knocked on the door and asked her by what authority was she speaking to the children and remind her of what happens to those who cause an innocent one to stumble. The millstone around the neck story is definitely something we don't want to talk about with a neighbor, right? Why are we ashamed of God's word? He said that not me!

Jesus was notorious for bringing the uncommon forgiveness balanced with uncommon reprimand. He rebuked his disciples when they turned away the little children. Remember? Not only did he rebuke them, He gathered the kids around Himself and publicly embarrassed the disciples by overruling their crowd control measures. Then, Jesus made a display of them further by taking the opportunity to preach a sermon about the importance of children and how they relate to the Kingdom of God. I imagine they were a bit red-faced and humiliated. But, I bet they never made the mistake of turning away children again.

Looking back, I should have stood my ground, too. Firmly yet lovingly, I could have activated God's Word in my life and on behalf of my children. Instead, I chose the popular and overused mentality of "let it go" or "love covers." I learned my lesson the hard way. Trying to be better than Jesus will never bring success.

I don't encourage you to go out looking for a battle. But when wrongdoing shows up at your front door - confront it. Stop pretending that you don't have the Answer. Truth is yours. The Way is yours. The Life is at your call. We have dominion in the earth because Jesus bequeathed it to us.

I am not suggesting that you and I go around pointing out all of the faults of those around us. We have enough of that taking place. But you owe it to those with whom God has called you into relationship. You owe it to them to walk the same line that Jesus did. Don't be selfish or false. Speak the truth in love, because you love, and because you love - you will bring correction when necessary. 1 Corinthians 13:6 says that love, "...does not rejoice in evil but, rejoices in the truth."

ᛒ

Jennifer Lopes is an ordained minister, and Co-Founder of A More Excellent Way Ministries and PULSE (Protecting Unborn Leaders Seeking Eternity). She serves alongside her family in ministry and is a devoted wife and mother. She enjoys serving crisis pregnancy centers and seeing young people find their identity in Christ. She currently resides in Mobile, Alabama, where she directs a national missions outreach. She can be reached at www.pulseprolife.com.

From Fear to Flight

by Pat Fenner

We all have fears. Whether it's fear of heights, fear of spiders, or fear of flying, in moderation and in appropriate situations, these fears can protect us. At other times, however, they become exaggerated and debilitating. And it is then that fear can keep us from living a life of excellence and achievement.

What is fear?

Looking back over my life, I think there were many times when I failed to attempt something because of fear. I was very involved in school – straight A student, active in extra-curricular activities, volunteer at my church and in my community, etc. My dad was a very well-educated man. While I was in high school, he encouraged me to apply to his alma mater, an Ivy League university. I didn't. I've always said that rebellion kept me from applying: I didn't want to be squeezed into a mold that I believed was being formed for me. While that may have been true to some extent, I now look back at that time and believe it was fear that stopped me. Fear that I wasn't really up to snuff; wasn't really everything everyone thought I was; wasn't really capable of the things that others expected from me. But there was also a fear that – God forbid that I should actually succeed! What if...I really was smart? I really could accomplish amazing things? I really could work hard and reach the lofty goals I often daydreamed about? And then...what or where would THAT lead?

Fear rears its ugly head in many different forms. I believe it is most clearly illustrated in the Biblical parable of the talents. This story, found in Matthew 25, describes a scene where a rich man is preparing to go on a journey, and entrusts his servants with his wealth. One of them received 5 talents (a measure of that wealth), the next, two talents, and the last, one. While the master was away, the one who received the most traded wisely and was able to double his amount. The second servant was also able to double his two talents, but the last servant did not fare as well. In fact, that servant "went and dug in the ground, and hid his master's money." (v 18) What we can learn from this story comes from an understanding of the last servant's attitude: his overarching fear was "What if I lose the coin?" Even with the little he had, he focused on the negatives. "What if I fail?" would be the question that would apply most to us. Upon his master's return, the servant sought to justify his inaction with a very wordy explanation, and one that, in summary, pinned the blame on his master! "...I knew you to be a hard man, reaping where you did not sow, and gathering where you scattered no seed..." (v 24) Because the third servant was afraid and hid what was entrusted to him, his master was not pleased.

What does fear do?

How many times in your life have you had a wild thought about a project or activity or career or invention or...but never moved ahead on it? Now think about what might have been going on in your head at that time. What thoughts were swirling around as you daydreamed?

For a few years after college, I worked at a major computer company. In that office there were many men and women with business degrees, many people who were seriously climbing up the

corporate ladder, many capable, competitive and career-minded individuals. Despite the fact that I had not trained for this environment and had no previous experience or inclination to work in the same, I found myself loving it – for a time. It was different, competitive, and surprisingly something new each day. People took their work seriously, and so did I. But after awhile, I started to study what it took to move ahead. Long hours. Extra job responsibilities. Extensive training. Off-hours travel. Commitment and sacrifice. Believing that I lacked the education and skills to get ahead, I started to question myself and my goals. Did I really have what it took? Although I had a manager who encouraged me and displayed great faith in my abilities and where I could go with them, I still had doubts - serious doubts - which ultimately crippled me. I continued to do my best at what I was assigned, but didn't seek more. I really think I was afraid to do what it took...afraid that if I failed to achieve the goals I had set, it would mean I was a failure. It was around that time that God began to bless us with children. And a short time later, I left the corporate world to take care of the home fires.

God in His mercy, however, has helped me to look back on that time and has taught me some valuable lessons on being a failure and feeling like a failure! There is a huge difference, of which I am most grateful. I believe this difference is best summarized by the difference in these two statements: "I could fail at this." and "I'm a failure."

"I could fail at this!"

This is a statement of fact that we all have to deal with everyday. You could fail at a myriad of things. You could fail at getting the dishes done. You could fail at catching up with the laundry.

You could fail at spending quality time with your spouse, or buying that birthday present, or getting to your "to do" list. Over the course of our lives we all fail at projects great and small. And sometimes it's easy to get discouraged. But for the most part, we are able to get up the next morning and start over with a clean slate. We are able to agree with Jeremiah, when he says "The… Lord's…mercies never come to an end; they are new every morning." (Lam 3:22-23) But at what point do we become paralyzed by the possibility of failure? At what point does that stop us from dreaming and planning and venturing forth? At what point does that cause us to bury our own talents?

This happens most often when our potential failure has the possibility of becoming public. When there is the chance that we can be viewed as a failure to the whole world; when we might appear foolish or stupid in front of friends and family, there is the possibility that our own definition of who we are can change dramatically. It is then, when our failure becomes public, that we risk believing that we ARE a failure.

"I'm a failure!"

Almost before we know it, this can become a "mantra" of sorts. And it was a very painful realization to discover just how quickly it became mine. Many years into my marriage, there was a period of time when my husband and I were undergoing counseling. We were going through a rough patch, but many of the issues had been recurring for years. For too many reasons to go into here, I had been taking all the blame for the problems and challenges that we were experiencing, rather than just admitting my part. In the middle of all this muck and mud, I discovered that I had started saying to myself that because of these troubles, I was a failure. And this belief started spreading to other areas of my life. I started believing I was a failure at parenting, a failure at friendship, but most disturbingly, a failure at doing whatever God had created me to do.

Fear will do just that. After it gets our eyes off-task and on self, it distorts our thinking. These incorrect and exaggerated perceptions leave us unable to move ahead. Fear, then, causes us to hide our talents and do nothing with them. We waste, and ultimately risk losing, what God has entrusted to us. We focus on the negative; on someone or something other than the task before us; other than what we are meant to do and able to accomplish (Phil 4:13).

What brings freedom?

So, how DO we move on? How do we get to the point of shedding our fears and soaring in flight? How do we begin to ask the question "What if I succeed?"

To begin with, it's important to remember that by failing to move ahead with the projects, plans or dreams that God lays on our hearts, we risk at least three things:

1)   Small vision – We can become so focused on ourselves and our "what if's" that we no longer look to see or meet the needs of those around us. Our bubble becomes smaller and smaller until we stop looking out the window and settle for looking in the mirror.

2)   A mediocre life – Defined as "of moderate or low quality, value, ability or performance", the results of living a life of mediocrity are best described in Revelation, where he who is neither hot nor cold... is spit out on the ground. (Rev 3:16)

3)   Hurting others – Did you ever consider that by not sharing whatever God has laid on your heart, whether it is a story or a lesson or a "better mouse trap", we may be withholding information that could actually benefit someone else?

My flight

So, having said all this I need to offer a bit of self-disclosure. This article has been sitting in my computer for about three years. It started out as a bunch of notes after a conversation with my husband. I'd work on it periodically, each time succumbing to a small nagging voice accusing me of being a fraud, a hypocrite, or at the very least, inadequate. But thankfully, in God's sovereign timing, and because of His grace and gentle prodding, you are reading it today. Written as much for me as for you, it is my hope and prayer that these words spur you on to overcoming whatever you've been afraid of; whatever is holding you back from stepping out and accomplishing the works He has created for you to do before time began. We were not created for bondage to anything less than service to our Savior and the glory to which He has called us. Realizing this, believing this and applying it to our lives will free us to soar to heights we may never have imagined, realizing accomplishments for our good and God's glory.

... those who hope in the LORD will ...soar on wings like eagles. (Isaiah 40:31)

Pat Fenner has been homeschooling her 5 children for 17 years, and writes on education and family topics on her website, Help 4 Your Homeschool. She reviews book as part of the Christian Women Affiliate "Review Crew", writes guest-posts on related blogs and contributes to Econobusters.com, an on-line magazine geared to frugal living. She is also part of the "Mother Knows Best" panel on Albany's (GA) Fox 31 TV morning show, Good Day. This is her first piece published in an anthology. You can reach her at www.Help-4-Your-Homeschool.com

LIKE FATHER, LIKE SON

by Mark Wyatt

(Excerpted from *"Hog Washed"*)

When I was growing up, television still showed cigarette commercials. In the midst of those, though, there was one public service spot that was particularly memorable. It showed scenes of a loving father and his little boy, around five years old or so. As the dad painted the house on his tall ladder, his little boy slapped on a few brushstrokes from his smaller one. As the dad drove the convertible and stuck out his hand to indicate a turn, the little boy did the same with his toy steering wheel and a hand out his side of the car. When dad washed the car with the garden hose, the son squirted water on the wheels with a water gun and wiped it with a rag. Each scene ended with a voiceover that said, "Like father, like son," with playful music in the background. And when they took a walk and sat under a tree, the father took out a pack of cigarettes, lit one, and then carelessly laid the pack between himself and the boy. And, of course, the son picked up the cigarettes, looked into the pack, then looked at his father, while the voiceover said, "Like father, like son? Think about it."

Of course with our great level of sophistication today, that spot seems quaint and old fashioned, but it was so powerful that it ran from September 1967 until 1982. That's 15 years of "Like father, like son." Why did it resonate so powerfully? Because it made people stop smoking? Probably not, though it might have made some parents think twice before laying a pack of cigarettes within easy reach of a five-year-old. No, its power was in its root message: "What the father does, the son will do."

Jesus said something remarkably similar in John 5:19. While being attacked yet again by the Pharisees for healing on the Sabbath, He said: "I assure you: the Son is not able to do anything on His own, but only what He sees the Father doing. For whatever the Father does, the Son also does these things in the same way." In that one incredible statement, Jesus essentially whisked us out of the audience and brought us behind the scenes of His entire earthly ministry. People had been following Him by the droves for years, watching Him do miraculous and wondrous works. But suddenly, Jesus does here what no good magician does- He revealed His secret. That's because He wasn't a magician, He was a Son! Jesus never intended to wow the crowds with great feats of prestidigitation, He was trying to model for us what would soon be available to us through the Holy Spirit. He was showing us what sons and daughters do! They live out of intimate relationship with God Himself.

This is the antidote to Christian Celebrity Syndrome. In our orphan hearts, not knowing or believing that we can have the same power of God that we see in our spiritual heroes, we follow them around like a suckerfish on a shark. The revelation of your identity as a son or daughter of God is the answer. When you see that your value is in who you are, not what you do, you will find that you no longer have the need to impress anyone. When the only person whose smile matters is the Father, you will find that there is really only one star on the stage– Jesus, the Only Begotten Son.

"EXORCISMS R US"

If you haven't read this story from Acts chapter 19 recently, here it is again, to perfectly illustrate our point:

> "God was performing extraordinary miracles by Paul's hands, so that even facecloths or work aprons that had touched his skin were brought to the sick, and the diseases left them, and the evil spirits came out of them. Then some of the itinerant Jewish exorcists attempted to pronounce the name of the Lord Jesus over those who had evil

spirits, saying, "I command you by the Jesus whom Paul preaches!" Seven sons of Sceva, a Jewish chief priest, were doing this. The evil spirit answered them, "Jesus I know, and Paul I recognize-but who are you?" Then the man who had the evil spirit leaped on them, overpowered them all, and prevailed against them, so that they ran out of that house naked and wounded." (Acts 19:11-16)

That probably shouldn't be one of my favorite stories in the whole Bible, but it is. This is our first recorded example of Celebrity Christianity Syndrome. These sons of a Jewish chief priest had obviously been convinced that what was happening through Paul was genuine. They had been following him around, taking notes, and measuring results. So, they did the next logical thing— they started their own exorcism business. The problem, though, is that they were only sons of Sceva, not sons of God. You see, this is what the orphan heart does. It watches what happens when a son of God relates intimately with the Father, bringing Heaven to earth. But all the orphan sees is cause and effect. Say this, get that. When in reality, a lot more had already been happening behind the scenes. As evidenced by the rest of Scripture, Paul was constantly praying, listening to the Holy Spirit, getting direction on what to do next. He never took for granted that he ever had a formula that would work without constant communication with the Father.

But Seven Sons, Inc. didn't see that part. They just saw the results and figured that they knew how to get them. And it didn't work. No surprise to us, really, but I imagine the epic failure of their business model came as quite a shock to them. And, even as we chuckle to ourselves, shake our heads, and tsk tsk their naivete, don't we do the same thing? Did you happen to see verse 12 above? It's the one that says that facecloths and work aprons that had touched Paul's skin were laid on the sick and they were healed. Have you ever just assumed that to be a formula for healing just because it shows up in the Bible? Don't get me wrong, I'm not saying God might not use that same method today. But it has to flow out of your intimate, hearing connection with the Father such that you know it is what He has said directly to you, for a specific time and a particular reason. You see, orphans see the results that sons get, then they try to formulate it so that it will work for them without going through all the steps of sonship—intimacy with God and hearing Him for themselves.

Let me show you how I recognized my orphan heart the same way.

NO SHORTCUTS

When I was a young man, I was greatly impacted by a number of great preachers, not the least of whom was the fiery Scottish preacher, Leonard Ravenhill. If you have ever read even a handful of pages in one of his books, or listened to just one of his messages, you know that Ravenhill pulled no punches. He could turn a phrase or level a gaze, and you knew that God was watching you. And, if you were even just a little bit open, the Holy Spirit would put his finger on your most sensitive hidden area and bring it into the light. The fact was, after hearing Leonard Ravenhill preach, you either marched away mad, or you ran to the altar in tears.

And so, as my friends and I began preaching, we knew we could do worse than to model our preaching after Ravenhill. The problem was, we weren't him. I doubt any of us spent a fraction of the time with God that Ravenhill did every day, and it never dawned on us that he had at least 50 years of wisdom, maturity, experience and unction on us, all put together. Still, that didn't stop us. We would go wherever we could— retreats, youth camps, country churches, downtown street corners— and deliver the fire. And to us, in our boldness, and even though we really loved Jesus and wanted people to know him, our measuring stick— mine, at least— was all wrong. I remember feeling that people could either get mad or get right, it didn't matter which. And if someone didn't tell me after the sermon that it really stepped on their toes, I hadn't done my job. Worse yet, just let someone tell me that they actually enjoyed it! What?!? Were they not even listening?

I acted as if the secret to Leonard Ravenhill's "success" was his cleverness, his delivery, his willingness to offend the hearer. And way too often, I succeeded in all of those areas. That was my orphan heart. Now, though, I see that the great power in Ravenhill's message did not reside in the pulpit or the page. It came from the prayer closet. It was birthed in tears and travail. Ravenhill paid the price to say what he said. I was wanting to have the same things he had in ministry, but I was trying to get it on credit and pay later.

Years later, after I had mellowed and matured a bit, I found myself pastoring a small Baptist church in Flower Mound, Texas. After about a year of pastoring there, much to my sincere amazement, we had not grown from 100 to 4,000 as I had expected. So, obviously, I had to find the secret to church growth. Lucky for me, not everyone was toiling in obscurity like I was, so there were plenty of church growth models to be had. At that time, two of the fastest growing churches in the country were Saddleback Church and Willow Creek Community Church under the leadership of Rick Warren and Bill Hybels, respectively. I had heard Rick Warren speak at a conference in Fort Worth a few years earlier, and was aware of the impact that Willow Creek was having in the Chicago area. So, I picked one. I obtained a video of Bill Hybels preaching a wonderful evangelistic message, and studied it. I memorized his points, his style, his jokes. I made replicas of his visual aids. Then, I scheduled a special evangelistic service on a Saturday night (the only cool time to have a church service in those days), and encouraged the people in my little church to invite all of their lost friends for an evening that would change their eternity!

The big night came, and I made sure to dress for success. I wore business casual pants, a blazer, and a shirt buttoned all the way up with a bolo tie. Very cool. I prepared, I prayed, and I waited for the throng. I opened the doors, and in they came! My wife, three of my church members, and one unchurched man brought by one of them. But I held nothing back. Clever illustrations, impressive props, and an impassioned plea filled the next 45 minutes. And at the end, the one lost man in the audience was absolutely, completely, unmistakably... underwhelmed. I believe now that it was because even though my intentions were pure, I was trying to fight a battle in someone else's armor. I was focusing on trying to formulate Warren's and Hybels' success, but what I missed was that they got their visions for ministry and for their cities directly from the throne, not from the copy machine.

When Paul said in 1 Corinthians 4:13, "Therefore, I urge you, be imitators of me," he was not saying "Dress like me, copy my mannerisms and idiosyncracies, and use my jokes." He was actually appealing to them as sons! Here is the same verse in context: "I'm not writing this to shame you, but to warn you as my dear children. For you can have 10,000 instructors in Christ, but you can't have many fathers. Now I have fathered you in Christ Jesus through the gospel. Therefore I urge you, be imitators of me. This is why I have sent to you Timothy, who is my beloved and faithful child in the Lord. He will remind you about my ways in Christ Jesus, just as I teach everywhere in every church." (1 Corinthians 4:14-17) Like father, like son. Even though Paul was unashamed to hold up his own life as an example, he was still pointing his spiritual sons in the house to the only Begotten Son, the One who said He and the Father are one: "[Timothy] will remind you about my ways in Christ Jesus..."

"Watch me," Paul is saying. "Watch me listen to the Father. Watch me as I magnify Jesus. Watch me follow the Holy Spirit. If I succeed, watch me point people to Jesus. And if I fall, watch me get up." And Paul said all of these things, not because these are the things that teachers say. These are the things that a father says.

THE THREE KEYS TO THE SEVEN WAYS TO THE FIVE SECRETS OF WHATEVER

It is good and right for us to seek new ways of breaking down complicated information and ideas into understandable, accessible bites that people can easily digest. There is a difference, though, between doing that and looking for the secret formula. I am wary of anything that offers me the "three simple steps" to whatever I am looking for if it has anything at all to do with my relationship with God. Those kinds of books and conferences appeal only to the orphan in me, looking for an easy way to the results I think I need to feel valuable in the Kingdom. It's like the spiritual version of yo-yo dieting. Millions of people have lost and gained the same 10 or 20 pounds year after year, because the idea of a quick fix is intoxicating. "I heard this minister pray this over a woman when she was healed, so that must be the phrase that gets God to move. Finally! I have discovered the secret of power with God!" And so we pray for someone in the same condition, and it seems nothing happens. And little do we realize that the minister we heard pray, has never prayed that for anyone before or since. It came from his communion with God and a well-honed, practiced ability to hear the Holy Spirit in that moment.

A couple of years ago, I was dangerously close to burnout. Some good friends of mine saw it and knew how to rescue me. Working with my church, they sent me on an eight-week sabbatical, to do nothing but get empty and rest— which, it turns out, is hard work at first.

At the end of week 2, I started a Sabbatical Journal. The Lord spoke something to me about what I was going through, then He was strangely silent until the end of the whole eight weeks. Here is my journal entry from that second week:

Monday, June 28, 2010

2:28 am

Ever since my first sermon at Loachapoka Baptist Church, and probably even before, I have been wearing someone else's suit. For the past 31 years, I have performed, both as a preacher and a pastor, in like manner of the best men that I had watched in that position. This has not necessarily been a bad thing, mind you, but still, I have modeled my pastoral style after those who have come before me. The problem, though, is that it has become Saul's armor for me. I have tailored my motivations, my goals, my preaching style, my counseling style, everything I do, to an idea in my head of what those great and godly men have done. But, in the final analysis, it isn't me. Somewhere inside all that armor is a David trying to get out.

So what is "me"? I have no idea. That is what I am going to spend the next six weeks trying to get to. My friend told me that this was going to be like peeling an onion, and he was right. I don't know how many layers I will have to strip away to find who I really am, but that is what I will do. Right now, I don't even know how to go about doing it, but I am confident that the Lord will reveal it. What's more, I don't really have a clue as to what I will find at the center of me, but whatever it is, that's who I will be. And that is what I will pastor from, preach from, be relational from, for the rest of my life.

I sure hope this works.

It did work. Not because I took eight weeks off. But because in that eight weeks, I rediscovered my identity as a son of the Only Living God.

I urge you, beloved sons and daughters of God— joint heirs with Christ and ambassadors of a greater Kingdom— shed Saul's armor. Stop looking for the magic formula. Just take your place as a son or daughter in the Father's house. Then take a deep breath the atmosphere of grace, believe that everything that belongs to the Father really is yours because of Jesus, then just walk into the living room, sit down on the couch, and stay there until you know who you really are.

Psalms in Poetry

By Keith Currie

(Excerpted from *"Psalms in Poetry"*)

Oswald Chambers, best known for his book My Utmost for His Highest, once wrote this: "The real reason for prayer is intimacy with our Father. There are many ways that help. To rewrite the Psalms into a free language of expression of one's own has proved to me a valuable treasure-house of self-expression to God."

One morning as I read these words, I was challenged to do this for myself, to rewrite the Psalms in my own expression as an enhancement of my own intimacy with our Father. I was reading through the Psalms at the time; so I began where I was in my reading—with Psalm 112. The thought to write it as poetry was my own idea.

So here it is. It is my hope that you enjoy, that you are encouraged and filled with hope, and that your own intimacy with our Father is deepened and enlarged.

PSALM 1

BELIEVE IT OR NOT

How well off the one who will not walk
In the wiles of the wicked.
So safe the soul that stands aloof
From sin's Deception Street.
The soul that seeks the truth that's sound
Won't sit in a scoffing seat.
How well off the one who will not walk
In the wiles of the wicked.

Instead, he delights in the law of the Lord
And makes it his meditation.
So like a tree whose roots run deep
Nearby the river's banks,
With timely fruit and leaf that's green,
He prospers and gives thanks.
Yes, he delights in the law of the Lord
And makes it his meditation.

The wicked are like the dust in the wind;
God's breath blows them away.

They'll fade from sight on Judgment Morn
When truth shines strong and bright,
For sinners cringe in righteous crowds
And hide from holy light.
The wicked are like the dust in the wind;
God's breath blows them away.

PSALM 2

WORLD PERSPECTIVE

Why have the nations gone so insane
And made their policies force?
And the people's plans are plainly vain;
They've chosen Failure's Course.

A summit's called for heads of state
To sit around the table.
Deceived by sudden rise to power,
They feel that they are able
To solve the problems without God
With treaties, pacts, and such;
But when the meeting's said and done,
It really wasn't much.

God sits in heaven and He laughs,
Amused at all their bluster.

Just South of Forever

From there He speaks His living-word
That leaves their plans afluster.

In purposed anger, He'll declare
That Jesus is the King,
The Son begotten before time
And from whom all things spring.

He'll place the nations in His hands--
Every single one.
His iron decrees will rule them all;
Their own laws come undone.

So kings, show wisdom; judges, learn
And tremble at His throne.
Show highest honor to the Son,
To Him and Him alone.

For wrath awaits those who refuse
To see Him as He is;
But blessing waits for those who yield
And gladly become His.

PSALM 91

SHELTER OF TRUST

He who lives in subjection to God the Most High

Will enjoy His protection, ever watched by His eye.

As a chick helter-skelters to its mother's spread wings,
So a soul finds the shelter that trusting God brings.

I proclaim Him as Maker, Protector, and Shield;
I trust the Creator, to Him gladly yield.

He delivers from snares; He delivers from death;
He protects, for He cares. Yes, He grants me each breath.

You will not be afraid of terror at night,
Of attack in the day or an arrow in flight,

Of the wasting disease that silently kills
Refusing to cease, destroying at will.

Though thousands may fall near at hand by your side,
Yet you will stand tall, clear of mind, open-eyed.

You've made God your hope; you trust the Most High;
You escape evil's grope--ever live, never die.

His angels will back you and you'll overcome
Though lions attack you, you will not succumb.

"He holds to me surely, so I set him free;
I promote him securely, for he has known Me.

"I will answer his call, be with him in trouble
I will not let him fall; his honor, I'll double.

"I will lengthen his days, a just compensation.
He has chosen My ways; he will know My salvation."

PSALM 139

PRESENCE

O Lord, You know me inside and out:
When I sit, when I rise, what I think.
You know what I do, You know where I live,
An intimate personal link.
You know what I'll say before I speak,
And You know what I'll never express.
I've learned that You're near;
Your presence surrounds;
I'm assured by Your hand's subtle press.

Such knowledge is wondrous!
I'm thrilled! I am awed!
For my mind cannot grasp who You are.
Where can I go from Your Spirit, Lord?
Where can I flee from the presence of God?

To heaven? You're there.
To the grave? You're there.
If I cross the sea with the wings of dawn,
You're there, You're there.
Even there Your hand will lead me
And Your right hand hold me close.
In darkness? You're there.
In the night? You're there.
Darkness and light are alike to You.
You're there. You're there.

In my mother's womb, You shaped and formed
Each detail that I am.
There's wonder and mystery in every cell;
And I thank You for who I am.
Your wondrous works are on display;
I see and I'm convinced
That I am made by Wisdom's touch,
Marked by Your fingerprints.
The moment when the sperm and egg
Were joined by intimate hearts,
Invisibly, skillfully, You designed
And chose my intricate parts.
You wrote the code for my DNA
With traits from dad and mum;
And then with laughter in Your eyes,
You added traits just for surprise--
The print of my Master's thumb!
In earliest stage, my course was mapped

Just South of Forever

And coded by Your hand,
Your purpose written in my heart,
My life designed and planned.

When I glean Your thoughts,
I gain and grow.
Such vast and varied store:
Such vital thoughts more numerous than
The sand upon the shore.
There are those who hate Your infinite thoughts,
And ignore that You exist.
Their hands are stained with the innocent blood
Of those who can't resist.
They speak against You and Your ways,
They swear Your name for spite.
Because I love You, I hate them.
O ban them from Your sight.
My hate for them intensely grows;
They have become my foes.

Take a thorough look at my sin-stained heart
And cleanse my internal depths.
Then freed from doubt and selfish taint,
I'll take eternal steps.

PSALM 145

FOREVER GREAT

I raise Your reputation ever higher.
I bless Your name forever and forever.
Every day I choose to bless You;
I will never cease to bless You.
I bless Your name forever and forever.

Says one generation to the next,
"The greatness of our God is beyond bounds."
We declare Your mighty acts;
Children learn your mighty acts.
The greatness of our God is beyond bounds!

We speak of Your awesome acts of power.
I will tell of Your greatness every hour.
Tell the stories of Your goodness,
Shout with joy for all Your goodness.
I will tell of Your greatness every hour.

The Lord is full of mercy and of grace.
Slow to anger, He is faithful in His love.
The Lord is good to all,
And His mercy's over all.
Slow to anger, He is faithful in His love.

Just South of Forever

Your godly ones declare Your acts of power.
Your godly ones proclaim their glorious King.
For Your kingdom's everlasting;
Your dominion's everlasting.
Your godly ones proclaim their glorious King.

When we fall, You are the one that lifts us up.
When we're bowed beneath our load, You raise us up.
We expect You to provide,
By Your hand we're satisfied.
When we're bowed beneath our load, You raise us up.

In all our ways we know the Lord is near.
He fulfills our deep desires when we draw near.
To those who call, He's kind.
In all His deeds, He's kind.
He fulfills our deep desires when we draw near.

My mouth will praise the Lord now and forever.
And all will bless His holy name forever.
Those who love Him He enjoys.
Those who fear Him He enjoys.
And all will bless His holy name forever.

Keith Currie

Keith W. Currie is an educator, poet, and songwriter currently living along the Gulf Coast in Mobile, Alabama. Previously published with Integrity Music for Kids, his best known songs are "Goliath" and "Jesus Was a Child Like Me." His first book of poetry is Psalms in Poetry: The Rhythm and Rhyme of Hope (Wyatt House Publishing, 2013), a work taking each Biblical psalm and rewriting it in modern poetry. He also serves as the principal of Covenant Christian School in Mobile. Visit him at www.keithwcurrie.com

CLOSING THE DOOR

by Ramona O'Brien

My mom called to tell me that since her brother wouldn't sell with her, she was going to sell her part of the house to him. His intent: to turn it into rental property. "I understand," I said. And I really do understand. She's tended and watched over that property since 1992 when Granny entered the hospital only to go "home" to the nursing home and not back to the house on Waring Avenue. Then, in January of 2000, 7 years after taking up residence in a place she never liked and could never call home, and 96 years and 4 days after the beginning her life well-lived, she passed into eternity. The thought that she was unable to return to her little house that she had called home and where she had "done" life for over 60 years made my heart twinge with sadness. My mom, after being caregiver for both person and property, and in grieving the loss of her own mother, needed to be able to close the door of one season and step through the door of another.

However, as much I understand all of that with my head, my heart aches at the thought of Granny's house not being "ours" anymore. Having become almost a sanctuary of sorts, a place to reminisce and re-visit a childhood that seemingly faded into the busyness of life – it would be that no more. Its existence would continue; my ability to have access to its existence would not.

So, I decide to make a weekend trip to TN in order to say goodbye to the house I literally grew up in. Sure, my parent's house on Highway 59 was home. But this was home as well. When I was young, Granny looked after me while my mom worked at the local bank. All day during the summers, after school during the school-year, and every Saturday in between found me at Granny's house. Saying that I spent a lot of time there was an understatement. I knew every inch of that yard, which measured more than an acre, I'm sure. I was well acquainted with the old house, inside and out, and I just couldn't let it go without saying goodbye. I needed to walk through the old house again, remembering the days, grieving the loss, smiling at fond memories, listening to sounds of the past.

I arrive and begin by walking around the yard, visualizing in my mind the way it looked many years ago. Back then, flower beds full of color were a familiar sight all over the yard, even surrounding the house. The large flower beds were over there, smaller ones there, the blackberry row over there, the strawberry patches there and there. A clothesline stretched from here to the fence. Now only ankle high grass and ill-kept flowerbeds fill the space.

Walking further back into the yard and turning, I notice that now only a few shallow sink holes mark the spot where the pecan tree, dignified and majestic, stood for so many years. The large pecan tree in the back yard had to have been at least 100 years old. Two people stretching their arms around the trunk as far as they could reach might be able to hold hands. The branches stretched far into the sky and reached out to cover almost the entire back yard. Back in the day, daffodils, iris, and other plants and happy flowers encircled the old tree. Granny could name each one. Then my attention turns to the apple tree near the fence row, source of many servings of homemade applesauce. The tree is weathered and twisted, yet I walk towards the tree and remember days filled with sunshine and laughter, picking apples and secretly climbing trees. And whatever happened to that huge crepe myrtle tree that was as tall as the house and showered the ground with pink flowers?

Returning to the front yard, walking up the steps and in the front door, I feel like an intruder, like I'm there without permission. Granny should be in the rocking chair in the front room. She's not. The house is somewhat out of sorts due to the fact that my mom has been going through everything in preparation for the eventual sale of the house. She seemingly has come to terms with all the emotions that are running rampant within me right now. Will I? I begin my farewell visit inside the house by walking through the rooms, opening doors as I go. In the front room the twin bed is missing, now strategically placed at my mom's for my son to sleep on during our visits home. I see more stuff out of its place, not right; it's all unfamiliar familiarity.

As I walk into the kitchen, a picture comes forth from my mind with such force that I'm taken back by the power of it. Granny is there, standing at the sink, washing the never-ending stack of dishes generated from her cooking, or baking, or canning, or whatever. Food is cooking on the stove, maybe a pot of beans, and a whiff of freshly baked biscuits just about to come out of the oven. I speak her name and the vision, the smells vanish, leaving me there alone with the dust, the musty smell of old grease, and the true vision of reality: the contents of the cabinets carefully stacked on the table, cookbooks and well-worn utensils here and there, the half-full garbage bag neatly placed against the back door. The harsh reality of the moment tears at my heart. All she worked for, all she lived for, down to this – a stack of old rusty pans and grease coated bowls, ready and waiting for the thrift store lady to haul it away for sale to strangers, or worse, to be throw away. Knickknacks that surely were special and held dear meaning for her, raise questions in our minds of "Where did this come from? Do you want it? Do you have room for it? But how can we throw it away?" Embroidered linens and handmade afghans, blankets, quilts, hand-sewn pillows and seat covers are in stacks in every room. How can you let this stuff go and pay homage to the memory of the one, who so painstakingly created so many of the items she used in everyday life? "Waste not, want not" seemed to be her lifelong conviction. Every scrap of material, every ribbon, every extra anything -- carefully tucked away "just in case". How do you move your memories from the tangible to the intangible; the seen to the unseen? At this moment, quite painfully, I think.

After wandering around and digging through a few boxes, I find a place to sit in each room. I take in what reality shows me and over-lay the memories of which piece of furniture went where and where Granny sat, and what I remember Granny doing and how she did it. It's too difficult to hold those thoughts for long. My mind keeps jumping to the present and the time allotment I have laid down for myself. I could stay here for hours, but no matter how hard I think, how much I want it to be so, I cannot bring her back. The time has passed for visiting and talking and laughing together. The time has passed for hugs, kisses on the cheek, and "I love you's." Oh, how I long for just one more visit with her. Time has passed too quickly. The things of true importance have slipped away.

It's now too late. Now is the time only for remembering and wishing and longing for the things that can never be again.

In that moment, how do you close that door and walk out, never to return? Well, you just do it. And that is what I do. I walk out the door, down the steps and make my way to the car, reassuring myself that all of my memories will continue to live on in my mind. Memories of a fiercely independent lady who gently wooed the ground for its harvest and devotedly loved her family with every ounce of her being, race to the forefront. I know that maybe those memories may actually be garnished by my imagination and the sweetening of time. Memories will remain. But the actual, physical ability to be in the origin of those memories, to touch, to smell, to "feel" the house and the life lived within it, all so important to me, will now be gone forever.

I return to Mobile, Alabama, heavy with the concerns of the weekend. I call my mom to let her know we are home safely and, lo and behold, she has "good" news. Her brother has decided to sell. He doesn't want to keep it for rental property. "I know you are happy to hear such good news," I say with complete understanding and partial whole-heartedness.

Gone. The house will really be gone soon. See, mom already has a buyer for it. He's only waiting to hear from her. I know she'll call him tomorrow and the old house will be one step closer to a stranger. Someone else will walk in the front door. Someone else will sit in the living room and watch their television, have their own family gatherings, oblivious to the past that lives on around them. Someone else will cook on the stove, stand at the sink and look into the back yard, keeping a watchful eye over small ones in their charge. They'll wonder why those sink holes are in the back yard and why that apple tree is still there. The flower beds and garden are now a distant memory for me, for my own mother and even the land itself.

Will they wonder about the one who lived there before them and what kind of memories were made right there where they stand? They probably won't care, but then again, maybe they will. Maybe they will make their own happy memories there. Maybe the house will once again be filled with conversation and hugs and wishes. Maybe they'll be blessed with the spirit of her contentment with life that continues to permeate those walls. Maybe they'll love that little old house the way she did. Maybe they'll care for the yard the way she did. And who knows? Maybe they'll resurrect the flower beds. I know the bulbs are waiting underground, waiting to surprise someone with a fresh bouquet and a smile.

CR

Ramona O'Brien, office manager for 18 years at Covenant Christian School in Mobile, AL, enjoys writing not only as a communication tool, but also as a leisurely diversion. As a child, Ramona spent many lazy summer days at her grandmother's house in West Tennessee. Memories of those nostalgic days prompted her to begin writing about the days spent with her granny. Ramona currently lives in Mobile, AL with her husband of 33 years. They have 3 grown children and enjoy the occasional game night, consisting of good food and a lively card game.

Wyatt House Publishing

You have a story.
We want to publish it.

Everyone has as a story to tell. It might be about something you know how to do, or what has happened in your life, or it may be a thrilling, or romantic, or intriguing, or heart-warming, or suspenseful story, starring a cast of characters that have been swimming around in your imagination.

And at Wyatt House Publishing, we can get your story onto the pages of a book just like the one you are holding in your hand. With professional interior design and a custom, pro-fessionally designed cover built just for you from the start, you can finally see your dream of being an author become reality. Then, you will see your book listed with retailers all over the world as people are able to buy your book from wherever they are and have it delivered to their home or their e-reader.

So what are you waiting for? This is your time.

visit us at

www.wyattpublishing.com

for details on how to get started becoming a
published author right away.

www.ingramcontent.com/pod-product-compliance
Lightning Source LLC
Chambersburg PA
CBHW072345090426
42741CB00012B/2930